Bill Shorten is the Leader of the Labor Opposition in the federal Parliament. He was born and raised in Melbourne, and is a proud Victorian. After completing secondary school at Xavier College, Bill graduated from Monash University in arts and law. Bill also holds an MBA from the Melbourne Business School. Having joined the Australian Labor Party at university, Bill worked as a lawyer at the firm Maurice Blackburn Cashman after finishing his studies.

Bill became involved in the labour movement in 1994 when he began work at the Australian Workers' Union as an organiser. Passionate about getting a fair deal for Australian workers, Bill became the AWU's Victorian Secretary and then National Secretary. Bill was also a director of Australian Super before entering Parliament in 2007. Bill served as a parliamentary secretary and as a cabinet minister in the Rudd and Gillard Labor governments.

Bill lives in Maribyrnong with his wife, Chloe and their three children.

FOR THE
COMMON GOOD
Reflections on Australia's Future

BILL SHORTEN

MELBOURNE
UNIVERSITY
PRESS

MELBOURNE UNIVERSITY PRESS
An imprint of Melbourne University Publishing Limited
11–15 Argyle Place South, Carlton, Victoria 3053, Australia
mup-info@unimelb.edu.au
www.mup.com.au

First published 2016
Text © Bill Shorten, 2016
Design and typography © Melbourne University Publishing Limited, 2016

Cover design by Philip Campbell Design
Typeset by Cannon Typesetting
Printed in Australia by McPherson's Printing Group

A Cataloguing-in-Publication entry for this title is available from the National Library of Australia

9780522869415 (paperback)
9780522869422 (eBook)

Acknowledgements

THEY SAY IT takes a village to raise a child. The same is true of writing a book. *For the Common Good* is the product of conversations, debate and argument with Labor colleagues and friends stretching back over many years. My values and beliefs have remained constant, yet I am indebted to my interlocutors for their insights and for helping to shape, challenge and sometimes even change my views on a range of issues. This book is very much the fruit of a collective endeavour. Entertaining the idea of writing it would not have been possible without the support and encouragement of Louise Adler at Melbourne University Publishing. My executive publisher Sally Heath and copy editor Meryl Potter were patient, sage in their advice and extraordinarily hardworking. The book is better for their labours. I would also like to express my gratitude to the many people who helped to make this book a reality. My sincerest thanks to Chris Bowen, Kim Carr, Greg Combet, David Feeney, Tim Harcourt, Mike Kelly, Bill Kelty, Richard Marles, Sharon McCrohan, Kaila Murnain, Tanya Plibersek and Chloe Shorten for their astute reading of various iterations of the manuscript. Thanks also to my staff, especially Nick Dyrenfurth, Ryan Liddell, James Newton and Amit Singh for their help in bringing this project to fruition. Any remaining errors of omission or fact are mine alone. Finally, I would like to thank my wife, Chloe, and our three precious children, Clementine, Rupert and Georgette, for putting up with the trials of living with an aspiring author and, of course, a parliamentarian. I love you all dearly.

Bill Shorten
March 2016

Contents

Introduction

'To be men for others'. These are the famous words of the Spanish priest Pedro Arrupe, SJ delivered in 1973 when I was just six years old. They have stayed with me.

As a child I didn't imagine that I would become a politician, let alone put myself forward as Australia's alternative prime minister. My first thoughts of a career turned to the vocation of social work. I'd volunteered as a teenager at school and liked what I saw. I enjoyed working with people. I loved seeing others empowered to strive to be better and healthier. And although I ended up working as a lawyer, as a shopfloor organiser, and then as the state and national leader of a large blue-collar union, the Jesuit dictum remained in my life. These five, simple, powerful words describe why I was driven to choose a life in national politics.

I became the leader of the federal Labor Opposition on 13 October 2013 and the first elected under the party's new rules that gave our members a direct say. I subsequently led the fight, inside the Parliament and within the community, against the

Abbott government's 2014 Budget, one of the most disgraceful and dishonest plans ever foisted upon the Australian people. Labor's campaign derailed that budget of broken promises and mean cuts—a result that was an unqualified good for our country. To give but one example: the proposed Medicare GP tax was a sheer betrayal of the Australian people.

Political parties and their leaders are defined by the institutions, standards and people they seek to protect and stand up for. As far back as 1893 Thomas Glassey, an Irish-born miner, auctioneer and reputedly the first Labor parliamentarian, put it so well in his speech to electors on 21 April. His party:

> wished to prevent the girl behind the counter and in the shop-room from being sweated. They wished to protect the child who was unable to protect itself from being robbed of its education in consequence of the impoverishment of its parents. The Labour Party aimed at elevating and not injuring, and at establishing the right to oppose—as far as in them lay—wrong.

Australians have a right to know what a newly elected Labor government will mean for them, their families, communities, workplaces and businesses. I want to lead a party—and a nation—of men and women for others. I want to see all Australians empowered to take control of their lives. I want every Australian to have the opportunity to fulfil their potential. I want to lead Australia to a better place. Labor people, taking their cue from our great prime minister Ben Chifley, call this 'the Light on the Hill'. I like to call this 'the Good Society'. It's my vision of a modern, smart, prosperous 'fair go' Australia where all of us have the opportunity to enjoy long, healthy, stable and meaningful lives. It is my dream of a country that provides renewed opportunity and equity to citizens who would otherwise be left behind. For a long time we just called this 'the Australian Way'. I'm convinced that the best way to protect our national achievement, adapt our population to the sweeping changes of our globalised

> *It's my vision of a modern, smart, prosperous 'fair go' Australia where all of us have the opportunity to enjoy long, healthy, stable and meaningful lives.*

world and seize new opportunities is through the election of a Shorten Labor government. My political motto is national interest first, party second, faction third, and any government I lead will govern in the interests of the nation as a whole.

The risk posed by a re-elected Malcolm Turnbull, and the Liberal Party he occasionally leads, will be catastrophic for working- and middle-class Australians. While the prime minister talks a different game to his predecessor and wears nicer suits, his agenda, such as it is, mirrors that of Tony Abbott. A Coalition government will hurt the economy, worsen the budget position and fail to create jobs or promote job security. It will lower living standards by running a de facto campaign to reduce wages. It will contribute to the end of the great Australian dream of owning your own home. A belief in increasing the GST lies deep within Liberal Party DNA. By contrast, it proposes tax cuts for high-income earners and multinationals. Medicare, our great nation-building institution, is again threatened. Education and science, two key drivers of our national prosperity, are no longer respected or

3

supported. Any talk about innovation without proper invest-ment in schools, universities and TAFE is just that—talk. Real climate change action is out of the question. Marriage equality and an Australian Republic have been placed in the too-hard basket. Malcolm Turnbull's dysfunctional government has no real agenda and is riven by infighting.

By contrast, the alternative government I lead has been busy identifying the challenges Australia faces today and in five, ten and fifteen years' time. We have consulted widely and have developed a practical, achievable plan for office, under-pinned by better paid and protected jobs, decent and affordable healthcare, better schools and universities, a fairer and more sustainable tax system, and action on climate change. Labor offers a positive plan for driving new economic growth and wealth creation as the mining–construction boom tapers off, a plan to reboot productivity and for infrastructure, a plan to create secure, well-paid jobs in an age of technological disrup-tion, and a plan to fix the Commonwealth budget. Labor will continue to zealously pursue equality for Australian women.

My plan goes much further: a Labor government I lead will again bring together the people of this nation—the men, women, children and families of our inner cities, suburbs, regions and remote communities; Indigenous, local and immi-grant; small and big business, workers and unions; young and old; progressive and conservative. It's time to move past the cycle of division that has characterised our politics for too long. At Federation in 1901, Australians consciously chose to unite under the name of the 'Commonwealth of Australia'. Our nation was born in a spirit of shared purpose, mutual respect and equal sacrifice. In 2016, we Australians must rediscover our ability to work together for the common good.

This book is my take on where Australia is right now, of our nation's place in a changing world, and the direction in which I believe it should be headed. This is not an exhaustive policy survey or manifesto, but more an insight into the thinking and values that inform my leadership. Australians are more astute than many in the media and politics assume. Presented with the facts, the arguments and a bit of respect, most people respond thoughtfully. I've seen it over and over again in the scores of negotiations I have handled in the workplace and now as a parliamentarian. This book is written in the same spirit. It gathers up my political story—from my earliest days in suburban Melbourne to what I now advocate as Labor leader. It's definitely not an autobiography. Rather it canvasses material that I've learned from thousands of everyday Australians journeying around the country and the many discussions I've enjoyed with friends and colleagues in and outside of the federal Parliament. Those conversations confirmed my faith in the special character and capabilities of the Australian people and the preciousness of our national achievement. *For the Common Good* is an invitation to share in my vision for a new century of Australian progress.

1

GROWING UP

XAVIER COLLEGE IS arguably Victoria's top Catholic boys' school, run by the Society of Jesus, also known as the Jesuits. Xavier's senior school is set on magnificent grounds in Kew, an old suburb five kilometres east of the Melbourne CBD. The school sits comfortably in the heart of Sir Robert Menzies' former seat of Kooyong. Xavier's list of old boys is long and distinguished: judges, writers, academics, entertainers, sportsmen and politicians—most of them conservatives. One of my oldest friends, John Roskam, was a fellow student there. John is a devoted Liberal Party member and for some years now has been executive director of the free-market think-tank, the Institute of Public Affairs.

The decision to send my twin brother Rob and me to Xavier was made almost exclusively by our mother, Ann, with the support of our father, Bill, a seafarer who had migrated from Tyneside in England (his full name was William Robert Shorten; I was given his first name and my younger brother was given his second). I remain forever grateful. We lived a fair distance from Kew, in Hughesdale, located in Melbourne's then growing south-eastern suburbs. My parents found the money to pay for our school fees, though there wasn't much left over. Throughout our childhood, I can recall our family taking holidays on only a handful of occasions. My parents worked hard to give my brother Rob and me the best start in life.

My mother, Ann, knew the value of a good education. It had transformed her life and she wanted the same for her boys. She was born into a blue-collar household in West Melbourne before moving to Ballarat, a regional city in central Victoria, and then East Malvern, the suburb where Rob and I attended St Mary's Catholic Primary School. Mum's father was a printer at the *Argus* newspaper and a union official; her cousin was Bernard 'Bert' Nolan, a long-time leader of the Seamen's Union. She took a teaching scholarship after school, taught at various state schools and then pursued a career as an academic. She met my father while on a holiday cruise to Guam in 1965. Dad was working as an engineer on the ship. His family also had a long history of union involvement at the Newcastle shipyards. After Rob and I came along in 1967, my father came ashore and set to work at the Duke and Orr Dry Dock in South Melbourne. I attended kindergarten at Monash University in Clayton, one of the earliest workplace childcare centres, where my mother held a part-time academic job.

Years earlier, Mum had been impressed with the Jesuit priests that she had met when she was a member of the Newman Society, a residential college the Jesuits operated at the University of Melbourne. As a cultural Catholic, a teacher and a school principal, she was taken with their approach to

8

education, so the Jesuits' school was chosen for us. Xavier was good for Rob and me—we were close, as twins usually are. We threw ourselves into debating, drama and sport. My brother had me covered on the sporting field. I was fortunate enough to win a place on the state debating team and took a shine to Australian history—devouring classic works by historians Manning Clark and Charles Bean—having come under the spell of a great teacher, Des King.

I'm sometimes astonished by how much Australia has changed over the course of my lifetime. My family got our first colour television, a Thorn, in 1976. It was a big deal. A few years later, Dad brought home a beta video recorder. Soon afterwards, the rotary dial telephone we had at home was replaced with a keypad model, which might soon itself be regarded as a museum artefact. Mum enrolled my brother and me in basic computer programming courses in the early 1980s, at a time when computers came in giant boxes and their screens were black with simple green text. These computers didn't do much: the Atari video game Pong was regarded as exciting. These days almost every waking hour of my kids' lives involves the use of some form of computer technology.

Outside the home, our community was changing dramatically. We were becoming more culturally diverse. White Australia was finally buried by the Whitlam government in 1973. Vietnamese families began moving into suburbs such as Hughesdale in the late 1970s, bringing with them what we at the time considered to be exotic cuisine. In 1978 the content on our TV changed forever when the Fraser government set up the Special Broadcasting Service (SBS), a radio and television station that ran programs and news in many different languages. At the same time, more and more women were entering the paid workforce and an increasing number were choosing to marry at a later age. A new wave of globalisation was beginning to make its mark on industries and jobs that Australians had taken for granted.

I grew up near the Chadstone shopping centre, known to Melburnians as 'Chaddie'. It was the brainchild of the retailer Ken Myer and, when it opened in 1960, Chaddie was the biggest of its kind. It was built on what had been paddocks owned by the Convent of the Good Shepherd. Back then it was just a covered walkway between the retailer Myer and other buildings. Hughesdale was reasonably well developed by the late 1960s, but progress came slowly. We lived on the corner of Neerim and Poath roads. It was a dangerous corner and for a long time was without traffic lights. On one occasion a car plowed through the front yard of our house. I vividly remember a fatal car crash and seeing the policeman removing the body of the driver who had been killed—it was the first time I had witnessed death. After that tragedy, the authorities installed traffic lights.

Our family lived in a modest Californian bungalow built between the two world wars. The family car, a Leyland 1500—a quirk of Dad's British heritage—rested in the driveway. The place had previously served as a small migrant boarding house for Greek migrants and was fairly run down. It wasn't a big house and, according to my mother, an entire migrant family had lived in each of the bedrooms. The house that had been home to those families and to my own is no longer there. After Mum moved out, it was knocked down and the site redeveloped.

Neighbourhoods felt smaller then. In Poath Road there was a small textile factory providing employment to locals. That's gone. There was a doctor's surgery where you had one GP, old Dr Wallace. That's gone. There was also a supermarket with just two aisles, a little single-fronted place where the second cashier only operated when things got really busy. Gone too. South Melbourne, the football club my father and I originally supported, no longer exists. Collingwood became my team when South Melbourne relocated to Sydney in 1982 and was reborn as the Sydney Swans. The Convent of the Good Shepherd next to Chaddie didn't last. When the nuns built the convent during the 1930s they hadn't executed the paperwork properly. When there was a fire there in the mid-1980s, the nuns were unable to keep possession of the convent as the insurance was too expensive, so Chaddie expanded—and it seems to keep expanding.

We went to church every Sunday morning—Mum and Dad insisted—at the Sacred Heart in Oakleigh, where the service was conducted in Polish. Bemused—Mum came from a long line of Irish-Catholic Australians—Rob and I would ask her: 'Why are we going to the Polish mass?' to which she'd retort, 'It's quick.' So I can claim to have been raised Polish Catholic in part. We didn't understand a word of what they were saying, of course. At one stage the non-Polish parish priest asked if Rob and I could assist him as altar boys. Mum refused point blank. She didn't like him. It was Father Kevin O'Donnell, an evil pedophile who was later arrested and convicted for abusing children. Mum's instinct was very good. Through her actions, Rob and I avoided a monster. He went to jail, but only after he destroyed countless lives. My parents continued to send us to a religious school and made sure we attended church regularly. Yet they retained a degree of scepticism towards organised religion. They thought we should go, but were themselves Christians who regarded attendance as a duty rather than the Catechism of the Catholic Church. Mum's two younger sisters had become nuns. Like other working-class girls of their generation they saw this as a path to education, though each subsequently left the convent and returned to secular life. I think Mum had an unresolved view of the Church—not of individual priests or the Jesuits—but of the institution and where it fitted in a modern Australia that was changing before our eyes.

Life was different in 1970s. More than 50 per cent of the Australian workforce belonged to a union, including my parents. There's been a gradual separation of people from many of the institutions that were around forty years ago when I was a 9-year-old: unions, churches and even political parties. I would catch two trains and a tram to attend school, and this was regarded as unremarkable for a young boy. No-one thought anything of getting the train early in the morning to Richmond, where various lines converged, and heading out again on a second train. The days were often long. I regularly caught late trains to get home. I wouldn't let my kids do that now, certainly not at the age at which I did, at 11 and 12. Many Australians feel that our suburbs aren't as safe as they once were, particularly for women. That concerns me. It's a big change, that personal loss of community confidence.

I got my first part-time job at 14, delivering pamphlets. Later, I held down a number of summer jobs and worked in a butcher's shop while at university. While some like to demonise young people, I see today's teenagers doing the same wherever I go—boys and girls on the verge of adulthood trying to earn some independence. It had taken me a while as a kid to work out what I wanted to do. The Jesuits placed an emphasis on community involvement and so I did volunteer work when I was at school. Visiting the kids at St Paul's School for the Blind and yarning with pensioners on a Friday afternoon was rewarding, so much so that I considered a career as a social worker. I'd also thought about following Dad and going to sea. I toyed with the idea of joining the armed forces and so enlisted with the Army Reserve. I clearly saw appeal in joining an institution that gave meaning and purpose to so many people. In the end, I settled on the law.

I had become attracted to the law in my late teens, having been guided in that direction by my mother. Her encouragement worked for my brother too. He signed up for economics/law while I did an arts/law degree. Mum had always wanted to train as a lawyer but didn't get the chance when she finished school. She was the eldest of four children and like many working-class women of her day she took up a teacher's scholarship. Her tertiary education was paid for by the government: the quid-pro-quo entailed teaching in the state system afterwards. The unfairness of missing out on her first option weighed heavily on her, I think. As we were growing up she completed a PhD and then embarked on a law degree. She completed that degree part time while she was working full time and raising a young family.

While I was attracted to the law, I was fascinated by work and workplaces. Attending the university kindergarten where my mother worked, I wondered what all these people were up to day after day in the imposing Robert Menzies Building, known as the 'Ming Wing'.

Dad was old fashioned and not hands-on domestically. His burst of parenting was on Saturdays. Sometimes he took us to the dock where he worked. This was where he rubbed shoulders with a remarkable range of characters. One fellow we met was known as Spider because he reputedly had eight arms in a fight. Dad was friends with Pat Shannon, the secretary of the Painters and Dockers Union, who was shot dead by criminals in a South Melbourne pub in 1973. I also remember the man who succeeded Shannon as secretary, Jack 'Putty Nose' Nicholls, coming to our house. Nicholls was found dead from a gunshot wound in his car in 1981. I wasn't close to him, although I remember his death being a big deal: front page of all the papers.

My father taught me about ships—he and my mother shared a love of them. When Dad took us to the dock I loved climbing over it. I enjoyed the feel of the place, full of colourful people, lots of intersecting tasks, mateship and, shall we say, boisterous conversation. That was when Australia had a commercial ship-repair industry. Over the years we've let that industry die, like too many others.

Dad was a smart bloke but also deeply frustrated. He grew up in the north-east of England during the devastating Great Depression of the 1930s. His story is an example of how an accident of fate and limited choice can change a life forever. Dad was, by his family's account, a bright kid. His father, Robert Shorten, a cinematographer, was—according to his family's recollection—rather hot-headed. He died from a cerebral hemorrhage in 1939 when my father was only 10, changing the direction of Dad's life forever. Dad won a scholarship to attend the Durham Cathedral School, yet he refused to go. He was bright but he simply didn't want to attend school any more. After his father's death, things got difficult for his mother, and money was tight. The job of raising my father fell to his maternal grandfather, Billy Cameron, a man who was steeped in the ways of unionism.

William 'Billy' Cameron was born in Dundee, Scotland in 1880. He served in the Royal Naval Reserve and worked as a stoker in the North Sea during the Great War. Billy told my father that he could hear exploding ships sinking during battles while he was below decks feeding the boilers—death would have come instantly if his ship had been struck. By 1936, he was a Jarrow Marcher, one of the unemployed coal and shipyard workers who marched from the north Tyneside town of Jarrow to London to protest against the devastating unemployment and poverty endured by working-class communities in the Depression's aftermath. He served as an independent Labour councillor, secretary of the Engineer's Union and chairman of the dockyard shop stewards. When he died, a long line of men queued up outside his house to pay their respects. He had been good at looking after people.

This was the man who influenced my father's upbringing. As a partial consequence, Dad didn't seek a formal education, but wanted to work on the docks with his grandfather. Aged 14, he dreamed of joining the Battle of the Atlantic in the service of the merchant marine during World War II. He was knocked back and two years later took up a trade. Apprenticed as a fitter and turner, Dad subsequently became a seafarer.

Mum always said Dad was an intelligent man. When he came ashore and married Mum, she made him get his chief engineer's certificate. He was street smart and possessed good people skills, but ended up taking refuge in the drink like many men of his generation. Looking back, Dad was probably depressed, but they didn't have counselling then. When I was 10, the same age he was when his father died, Dad suffered a heart attack. It hurt seeing that. No child should ever have to see their father so vulnerable at that age. Yet it changed him. He stopped drinking as much, which was welcome, although he developed a shorter fuse. Why? I suppose it shocked him—he was only 47—but maybe he was experiencing pain, too. He'd smoked a lot and drunk a lot, to the point that his health was less than wonderful. If you watch old cop shows from the 1970s and see the blokes with big fat ties and the cigarette ash spilling down their jackets, that's the world my Dad inhabited. This time left an indelible mark upon me. Dad would take my brother and me to the football to see the Swans on Saturdays. He'd be dressed in his big woollen overcoat, park us in the grandstand, and go off to meet his mates and drink beer. I guess for him it was an escape of sorts. It was this lifestyle that contributed to his premature death.

My mother was always motivated to do well. She was the first member of her family to attend university. She went down the path of taking a teacher's scholarship because there was not enough money in the family or sufficient support and encouragement for her to attend university to study law as a young woman. If you look at the stories of my parents, in each case I can't help but reflect on how chance and timing, social class and lack of money changed the direction of their lives.

Mum's first missed opportunity drove her for the rest of her life. In Dad's case, his missed opportunity led to choices that made him a more frustrated person than he might otherwise have been. I'm convinced that the experiences of my parents— the opportunities they were unfairly denied or in Dad's case didn't fully grasp—have pushed me to ensure that people get the chance to achieve their full potential.

What we say to each other in families can have such a damaging impact. Mum told me that her self-confidence took quite a hit when she was a teenager. She was on her way to her school formal, all dressed up and probably a bit nervous and excited, when she came upon her father at the railway station. He was drunk and said some awful things to her. I know less about my father because his extended family lived on the other side of the world, and his story was more difficult to delve into. It seems that while he had some positive early role models, he probably had to bring himself up at various times. I think that Dad's personal disappointments pushed him away from us as a family. Dad was an old-fashioned father—he grew up during the Depression after all. I can't pretend there wasn't conflict at home. Dad was never physically violent towards Mum, but there were plenty of arguments and, looking back, I can see that a permanent undercurrent of tension persisted in our home life. I don't want other children to experience that in their formative years.

Dad and Mum divorced when I went to university; he later remarried. My brother and I maintained a relationship with our father for a few years, but that eventually fell away. Thankfully Dad and I reconciled. I went to see him and invited him to my wedding to my first wife, Debbie. He accepted, which was a big deal. Dad never did make it to the wedding: a week later, aged 70, he died of another heart attack. I regret not asking Dad more about his life. As with most family histories, you only start to think about it when the eyewitnesses are all gone. I'm sad Dad wasn't in my life for such a long time and I'm sure he felt the same way about me too. You should never ever leave conversations unsaid if you can avoid it.

It couldn't have been easy for my parents, raising twins. I didn't appreciate it enough at the time. I'd come home from Xavier and say to my parents,

Mum taught me that merit is the measure by which we should all be judged— not birth or gender, or the accumulation of wealth.

'Mum, why can't you just be in the tuckshop like other mums?' or 'Why does everyone else have a new car and our car's old and battered?' You don't always cover yourself in glory as a kid. Mum and Dad always made sure that I understood that you don't forget where you come from—it's not someone's material wealth that's the indicator of who they are. My parents' values live with me. They did the best they could for us as parents. That's all you can ask. It's a tough job, balancing the demands of work and family.

Being a dad has changed me for the better. Chloe and our three kids—our younger daughter Clementine and Chloe's two children from her previous marriage, Rupert and Georgette— have taught me so much. They keep me grounded. Like all parents we are protective of our kids. A child's innocence is precious, but the nature of my job and our modern, digital world throws up unique challenges. I wish it wasn't so.

There is dignity in work. My parents encouraged my brother and me to take up a trade if we wanted or pursue a white-collar job—it did not matter. They were simply committed to us getting a good education, wherever it took us. They also imparted to Rob and me a healthy scepticism—that you should always think for yourself. Each Sunday morning, we heard the thud of the *National Times* hitting the front porch—this was a newspaper that investigated corruption with its pithy, cheeky take on politics. Out on the kitchen table, Rob and I would pore through the pages and laugh at the Patrick Cook cartoons. We were encouraged to watch the news on television from a young age. The world looked like an interesting place to me. I was curious and optimistic.

Both sides of my family were Labor people. However, the experience of the Whitlam government shook my parents. I think they were disillusioned with Labor for a while. There was a period in the mid-1970s where, like all working people, they were concerned about where the Australian economy was heading, what it meant for them and their family, and wondered if Labor had always made the right calls. Their moment of doubt passed quickly. Mum came from a family of tribal Labor supporters, even if, as proud Australian Catholics, the Great Labor Split of the 1950s had frayed that relationship somewhat. A lot of the union men in Mum's family clung to old-fashioned attitudes towards women and I know that annoyed her. Yet my parents were always union people—always for workers.

Mum used to tell me that her father was a smart fellow. Richard 'Dick' McGrath was a printer by trade, shifting from lithographic to gravure printing over time. He'd seen technological change and, after returning from military service in World War II, Dick retrained himself so he could take advantage of the economic opportunities of the postwar years. That's a lesson about change I've always carried with me. I would see factories close, shops close. Yet new opportunities also arise. During the 2015 ALP National Conference, I took a few moments to walk out of the venue, the Melbourne Convention Centre, and walk along the adjacent Yarra bank. I strolled over to the National Trust's Polly Woodside, a 130-year-old tall ship that's permanently moored next to the Convention Centre as a tourist attraction. The Polly Woodside sits right where the Duke and Orr Dry Dock used to be. Forty years earlier, I'd been running around this place, awed by the size of the ships and the hard work being done there by the men on the job. Now I was here in this thriving hub of restaurants and retail, doing my work as Labor leader.

In April 2014, Mum passed away suddenly, aged 79. She continues to be my inspiration. She grew up in a working-class household that was political—her Uncle George McGrath was a railway worker at Spotswood and an active delegate of the left-wing Australian Railways Union—and saw education as the path towards self-improvement. When Mum was awarded a scholarship to undertake a Bachelor of Arts at Melbourne University, she paid her own way and gave the proceeds to her parents, who used them to pay for the schooling of her younger siblings. This was in the early 1950s, when it was uncommon for working-class people, let alone women, to study at university. She was undaunted. The social barriers that she must have encountered during this time only served to reinforce the no-nonsense style that she carried throughout her life. She

20

expected people to make an effort and to work hard. She was always trying to learn something new. Mum collected a BA, a Diploma of Education, a Master of Education, a PhD, an honours degree in law and the Supreme Court prize in law. That last one stirred a mixture of great pride and minor embarrassment on the part of Rob and me, because she was awarded the prize in 1985, our first year as law students at Monash. It was an incredible achievement for someone with a full-time job, twin teenage boys and no family connection to the legal profession.

My mother taught me that it was possible to be proudly Australian—to be patriotic in the sense of loving one's country and wanting it to be better—yet also embrace an internationalist view. Before Mum was married, she was an inveterate traveller. She wanted to see the world and she did throughout her life—Spain, the Rocky Mountains, Newfoundland, Korea, the pyramids in Egypt, Paris and the Panama Canal. It became a regular activity for her family to travel to Station Pier in Port Melbourne to see her off on another journey in a blizzard of streamers thrown from the wharf. Here was a woman of working-class stock expanding her horizons. She used these journeys to gather knowledge. You and I might know that the Eiffel Tower was built by a man named Eiffel. My mother would know its cost in francs, how much it weighed, why it was built and what the government that commissioned it thought of it. Mum wanted to understand things as completely as she could. Her job as a schoolteacher and as a school principal took her places too. She taught at Orbost and Queenscliff in country and coastal Victoria, and in the inner-Melbourne suburb of Collingwood, as well as further afield in Townsville and London.

This was the woman who raised me. These were the stories that I grew up with. Her example had the greatest impact on me as I navigated my little world of Hughesdale and then Xavier and Monash. Mum taught me that merit is the measure by which we should all be judged—not birth or gender, or the accumulation of wealth. Merit is defined by hard work, attainment, taking responsibility and doing the right thing. She taught me that personal ambition goes hand-in-hand with looking out for and making sacrifices on behalf of others. Through her experience I learned that change should be embraced, but it was important to remain questioning—to retain a healthy scepticism of the reasons advocated for change. I will be forever grateful to my mother for these gifts and the many ideas and the example she passed on to me. I miss her every day. I wish I could tell her that.

2

A LABOUR OF LOVE

I HAVE BEEN A member of the Australian Labor Party for thirty-one years. I have met and worked with many people who were politicised by the 'It's Time' election of 1972, when the ALP, led by Gough Whitlam, won office for the first time in twenty-three years. Other Laborites were motivated by the events of 11 November 1975 when Governor General Sir John Kerr dismissed Whitlam's reformist government. An unelected, unaccountable man had no right to sack a democratically elected prime minister by stealth. My political awakening came an electoral generation later. In 1982, John Cain's Victorian Labor Party ended twenty-seven years of Liberal government. Then, as I was beginning my Year 11 studies in the heat of late summer in 1983, Malcolm Fraser called a snap election on the same day that Bob Hawke took over as Labor leader from Bill Hayden. The country was in the depths of its worst recession in half a century; Australians were yearning for an end to the bitter divisions that Fraser had set in train seven and a half years earlier. On the back of the campaign slogan 'Bringing Australia Together', Hawke led Labor to a comfortable election victory. Hawke's prime ministership, working in tandem with his treasurer, Paul Keating, has influenced much of my subsequent thinking. Indeed, Hawke's consensus style was not only suited to the times but spoke to the best traditions of our nation's political history.

Australia's success as a new nation in the years after federation is a testament to the ability of Labor people and small 'l' liberals from the other side of politics to find common ground. Some of the best examples were the federal Parliament's passage, in 1904, of a *Conciliation and Arbitration Act* to resolve industrial disputes, and the Commonwealth Court of Arbitration's establishment of the living wage three years later: the Harvester judgement, which linked a fair day's pay with industry assistance. Then there were bold initiatives, such as the introduction of welfare initiatives—pensions and a maternity allowance—and agreement on matters of immigration and national defence. The journalist Paul Kelly calls this set of policies the 'Australian Settlement'. It was a heady era of nation-building that peaked once Labor took office in its own right (1910)—a world first by the way. Prime Minister Andrew Fisher's Labor government founded the Commonwealth Bank and the Royal Australian Navy, chose Canberra as the nation's permanent capital, and began the building of a transcontinental railway linking Western Australia to the eastern states.

This was the tradition that Hawke identified with, even if he reformed many of its key policy planks. It was how he worked as ACTU president and then as prime minister. Hawke staged a national economic summit in his first weeks of office, a gathering that drew together leading figures from industry, finance, the welfare sector, unions and state governments. Watching it all unfold in the newspapers and then discussing it in class was a thrilling experience for a political nerd like me. Most of all, I was impressed by the consensual way in which Hawke led, his way of bringing people together; of uniting the nation rather than playing groups off against each other; repudiating extreme solutions;

the Third Way is really the Australian Way—the relentless pursuit of economic efficiency with fairness always in mind.

and the coming together of employers and workers. The Hawke Labor government changed Australia forever and for the better. The nation opened itself up to the world. The dollar was floated in December 1983; restrictions on foreign investment were eased; and tariffs were reduced.

The Hawke/Keating mission was guided by the better angels of Australia's nature. Labor believed that government could make bold economic decisions and harness market forces while preserving the nation's egalitarian soul. Consensus and proper cabinet government were crucial. Hawke implemented an Accord to tackle the twin scourges of unemployment and inflation, in partnership with the ACTU secretary, Bill Kelty. In return for exercising wage restraint, Australians were provided with a raft of social wage increases—the reintroduction of universal healthcare in the shape of Medicare; compulsory superannuation, which has built one of the largest pools of savings in the world in just a quarter of a century; and an expanded higher education system funded through income-contingent loans that is now used in many other countries and contexts. The *Sex Discrimination Act* was created, making it illegal to discriminate against women on the basis of their gender. The Hawke government saved the Franklin River in Tasmania. Another great Labor achievement in these years is often passed over. The Hawke government's response to the AIDS crisis that hit Australia in the mid-1980s—scaremongers called for the segregation of those with the disease—became the role model for other countries.

All this amounted to a new Australian settlement for new times and it was done the Labor way. It's why Australia avoided the brutal free-market excesses and union-bashing of Thatcherism in Britain and what in the United States became known as Reaganism. Australian Labor invented what Bill Clinton, Gerhard Schroeder and Tony Blair later called 'the Third Way', the rallying call of modern social democrats across the globe. As the economist Tim Harcourt argues, the Third Way is really the Australian Way—the relentless pursuit of economic efficiency with fairness always in mind. The Australian Way works, yet it is not set in stone. Once again, people are telling us we have to prioritise either the economy or the society. It's a false dichotomy. Unless we want to risk the Australian way of life and end up with the lack of social mobility that we see in Britain and America, Labor has to prevail in today's battle of ideas—just as Hawke, Keating and Kelty did in the 1980s and 1990s. I'm fortunate that, as Labor leader, I am able to pick up the phone and seek the advice of these and other nation-building giants.

Hawke's approach to politics resonated with me. In Year 12, aged 17, I tried to join the ALP. It was quite the ordeal. The government I saw in the media looked so modern. The party I attempted to join seemed the opposite. It became clear that Labor was built upon a structure that was designed in the 1890s, of inflexible, physical meetings. It was also based upon the assumption that politics was a form of men's business: the idea that men can simply go out in the evening. In Hughesdale, we were represented by two Labor members: Race Matthews at a state level and Joan Child federally. The party's response to my initial inquiry about membership was that I could come and see them between 9 and 5 to talk about joining. I wrote back that I was in Year 12 and I couldn't miss school. Could I meet someone at the weekend? The message came back: the party didn't do weekend meetings. So I didn't join Labor during my school years: I had to wait until early the next year. My paperwork was formally approved on 3 March 1985, during my first week as an arts/law student at Monash University. I'm pleased to say that today you can join the party immediately online.

My interest in politics had its roots in my childhood exposure to my parents' workplaces, seeing how people went about their business and interacted with each other. Workplaces are inherently political places and relevant to how we organise ourselves socially. That was the appeal from where I sat—it's no accident that it led me to a working life within the two branches of the labour movement. By the time I approached the end of my law degree I knew that I wanted to work for a union. I completed my degree, but the law hadn't grabbed me. It wasn't looking like a long-term career. During my time at university I had been active in the youth wing of the ALP and worked part-time jobs in MPs' offices, being mentored by the likes of Cain government Industrial Relations Minister Neil

Pope and Senator Robert Ray. This only reinforced my views on the positive role that unions play in our nation. I believe in merit and fairness, that everyone deserves a go, and that we need a balance of interests rather than the domination of a single interest in our workplaces. Unions seemed the best way to advance those ideas. Being an official in a blue-collar union was an excellent expression of what I knew about Australian history and about social justice.

I wasn't quite finished with the law. I didn't want to throw away several years of study, the nights memorising case law and learning advocacy, so I committed to doing my articles. I also felt that I owed it to my mum to do my articles, get formally qualified, and spend time as a practising lawyer. So I joined Maurice Blackburn, a leading workplace and social justice law firm founded by the Labor politician of the same name. All the while, I was looking ahead to joining a union, finding out more about how the economy worked, how it all fitted together. I wanted to work in a moderate union, one that identified with mainstream Labor.

My teens and university years coincided with the final stages of the Cold War—the uneasy, long-running stand-off between the United States and the Soviet Union overshadowed life then. Nuclear weapons and disarmament were big issues. I didn't believe in unilateral disarmament. The Soviet Union was an ugly dictatorship, not a romantic utopia. I was impressed by Lech Walesa, the leader of Poland's Solidarity, the trade union born of the Gdansk shipyards. Resisting Poland's dictatorial communist leaders was brave. The fall of the Iron Curtain and the demise of the Soviet Union liberated millions from a horrible system. I saw its aftermath up-close as a backpacker on the trans-Siberian railway.

After working with Maurice Blackburn under John Cain, Jr for eighteen months, I started to look for a position with a moderate union. I was offered a job as the national lawyer of the Transport Workers Union but knocked it back. Many people with legal qualifications become industrial advocates or research officers before moving on to leadership positions. I didn't want that: I wanted to be an organiser. I didn't want to be a lawyer in a union. I wanted to get into workplaces alongside people who were trying to make a living. I wanted to get more people involved in the union. I had worked out that the hardest job in a union was organising non-unionised worksites. I had been gripped by Australia's experiences of the 1890s, when the colonies experienced a devastating depression that brought mass unemployment and poverty to working people—and saw unionised workers organise themselves into what we now know as the ALP. I knew that Labor's earliest leaders had come up through the union ranks. Andrew Fisher, Labor's first great prime minister, worked as a coal miner in his native Scotland and served as a local union official. The prime minister who courageously led this nation through the trials of World War II, John Curtin, had spent years travelling around the backblocks of Victoria signing up members to the Timber Workers Union. Chris Watson, the first Labor prime minister in the world, Jim Scullin, who governed during the turmoil of the Great Depression, and the engine driver turned nation-building prime minister, Ben Chifley, all served the union movement in some capacity before entering Parliament. They were all interested in people. That was the impulse that drove me too: how people work, earn a living, save and create a good life. In 1890, a group of Sydney unionists outlined the necessity of forming the New South Wales ALP. It wasn't about a particular policy or a grand ideological mission. Rather, in their words, it was 'to ensure to every man, by the opportunity of fairly remunerated labour, a share in those things that make life worth living'. Such thinking drew me to the labour movement.

It was as I had hoped. In 1994, when I was 27, Bill Kelty encouraged me to become an organiser with the Australian Workers Union, the oldest continuous and most distinguished of our nations unions, under the auspices of the ACTU's innovative *Organising Works* program. For the next thirteen years, the AWU gave me an up-close look at the lives and aspirations of Australians working across an extraordinary range of occupations, up and down the width and breadth of the continent. Being a worker's compensation lawyer had been character building. I was helping people, but when you're dealing with people in the legal system, they have already suffered, often immensely. I could get them some money and try to redress the wrong that had been done to them. It was remedial, however, not preventative. As a unionist, I found I could actually help prevent unfairness and injustice. Importantly, unionists could make things better by working in a meaningful, co-operative way with employees and employers.

Some of what I saw in my childhood drove a desire to prevent bad things happening rather than acting after the event. I watched my maternal grandfather die slowly after he suffered a shocking stroke when I was in Year 9. He was treated at the Alfred Hospital in Melbourne's inner south and was hospitalised for six months. He just sat there. He couldn't speak. All he could do was stroke his eyebrow. It was a big thing to see him felled.

As an official of a union that represented many people who perform hard physical work, the hospital visits continued. One visit involved a member, a big, fit New Zealander. A bobcat had tipped forward in the trench he was working in and cut off his legs. I visited him a few times in the rehabilitation hospital in Caulfield. These experiences seared into my consciousness the reality of horrible, life-changing events at work and how people cope afterwards. How do we stop these horrific things happening again? What does our society need to do to give them a chance of leading a manageable and meaningful life? We know how to look after them in the acute phase, but subsequent care and rehabilitation is another matter.

During my time with the AWU I raised money for the families of jockeys who died riding. I had a member working in a factory who lost his arm at a pinch point in a poorly fenced-off machine. Another member's lungs were scarred when an explosion took place in the non-ferrous furnace he was working on. The fumes and smoke poured out. As he breathed them in, his life was transformed instantly. During my years as a young organiser, a shop steward I had just recruited was killed at work, crushed by a vehicle at a Keon Park factory. Twenty-one years later I can remember his name: Graham Baker. An explosion at the Esso gas plant in Longford, Victoria in 1998 killed two men; another two were badly burnt. These tragedies could have been avoided through close cooperation between employees and employers, and a robust role for unions.

When I joined the AWU as an organiser I wanted to experience the full breadth of the Australian working experience. I wasn't disappointed. I organised ski fields and worked to get up an agreement for the tow operators and ski instructors. I looked after fruit pickers, visiting packing sheds along the Murray. Our membership was wide: winery workers, greenkeepers, forklift drivers, steel and shipyard workers, stable hands and shearers, as well as health, retail and hospitality workers covered by the Queensland branch. I used helicopters to visit members on oil rigs in the Timor Sea and to visit ship operations in the Bass Strait. I've been underground in mines across Australia. I've organised embalmers, coffin makers and car assembly workers. I know how we make wind turbine blades and glass. I've stepped into every sized aeroplane in Australia and seen them stripped down when they're getting their major overhauls, because I looked after the engineers. I journeyed to the top of cement silos with crane drivers, travelled into sewers and represented forest firefighters who protect people and properties during dangerous bushfires.

For Labor, a strong safety net for Australian workers, including a decent minimum wage, is non-negotiable. The argument that a strong minimum wage causes unemployment just doesn't stack up.

I loved my organising years. But at age 30 I was presented with the opportunity to enter state politics, with the chance of running as Labor's preselected candidate in what was regarded as the safe seat of Melton at the next state election. If I had entered the Victorian Parliament in 1999 I would have worked in the terrific government of my friends and mentors

Steve Bracks and John Brumby. I wasn't sure I was ready to give up my role organising, so when rank-and-file AWU shop stewards got together and asked me to stay, I handed back my endorsement. In 1998 I was elected secretary of the Australian Workers' Union, Victorian Branch. I never regretted the decision. I spent another nine years with the union—in 2001 I was elected the AWU's eighteenth national secretary, serving in that role from 2001 to 2007, as well as on the executive of the Australian Council of Trade Unions. This was an era when the labour movement faced the fierce pressure of the Howard government's anti-worker, anti-union agenda: from the *Workplace Relations Act* of 1996 to the ugly scenes of balaclavas on the wharves during the 1998 maritime dispute and later the radical *WorkChoices* regime.

Those extra years taught me so much. As Labor leader, I still think like an organiser. Whether it's dealing with the rising influence of vested interests or solving a community-level problem, empowering people is the key. Relationships are crucial: get people to come together, define their position and work from there. Don't begin with a pure ideological solution. Take account of all viewpoints. When everything is done on a more equitable basis you creating better outcomes. I learned a lot on the way to entering Parliament, meeting so many thousands of workers. I was honoured to negotiate on their behalf and to be there for men and women in tough times. More than anything, the experience gave me a lifelong respect for the working people of Australia and confirmed to me all that was good about our country. If I needed to get a gas plant working, it would be no good ringing a highflyer at the company's head office. It is the workers on the job who know how to do it, who get things done. All too often that's forgotten or conveniently ignored.

I am proud of my union past. There are 1.8 million union members in this country, the largest social movement in Australia. They belong to a movement that can claim a large share of the credit for building the Australian Way: our generous safety net—including penalty rates—and decent conditions at work; the small matter of the weekend; annual leave and sick pay; compulsory superannuation. There is no way of building a common good without the active participation of working men and women, and their unions are an undeniable force for good. William Spence, co-founder of the AWU, explained it well a century ago in *History of the AWU*:

> The man who joins the Union becomes a better man. He becomes more social, takes a wider interest in human affairs, and consequently becomes more unselfish. His membership makes him a better husband, a better father, a better and more active citizen.

The Coalition is incapable of understanding this view. It seems intent on smearing my past, most notably through the extraordinary and, for taxpayers, expensive royal commission into trade union governance. I regard some of the attacks made upon me at the commission's hearings as bizarre. They were political and they are personal. They were and are an attempt to destroy the Labor Party, unions, my leadership and even former leaders. Justice Dyson Heydon's intervention during my testimony to the commission revealed that the commission was unable to operate free of perceived political bias. My judgement of bias, and that of many others, was confirmed by Heydon's decision to accept—and then belatedly withdraw from—a speaking engagement at a Liberal Party fundraiser. It was also disrespectful to hear about the commission's decision to formally clear me of any wrongdoing indirectly via a late Friday night media release. Above all, the royal commission was an insult to the ordinary men and women whose involvement in this nation's union movement is guided by a noble objective: to be men and women for others.

To be clear, I have zero tolerance for criminality or corruption wherever I see it. I'm bitterly disappointed by any report of corruption in the union movement. That's because a strong union movement is so critical to protecting conditions that Australians have fought long and hard for and so many Australians rely on every day—like decent pay, safe workplaces and penalty rates. No one has a stronger reason to stamp out any corruption in the union movement than the Labor Party. As Workplace Minister during the Gillard government I intervened to put parts of the troubled Health Services Union into administration. As Opposition leader I have proposed new whistle-blower protections and doubling the penalties for individuals who do the wrong thing. It's because I care about unions and will always respect the work they do that I'm determined to uphold their integrity. Labor is anti-corruption across the board; the Coalition is simply anti-union and anti-worker.

When I joined the AWU in 1994, Australia was still emerging from a deep recession. The industrial relations sphere was undergoing revolutionary change. The last pillars of the original Australian settlement were being renovated for the world of the twenty-first century. The Keating government had taken the first steps towards enterprise bargaining, which meant unions were more engaged in direct negotiations with employers rather than subject to centralised wage fixation overseen by the arbitration court. Only a year earlier, the unemployment rate sat just under 11 per cent, which represented almost a million men and women out of work. The economy was being opened up to more competition. The key to the future prosperity of Australians was increasing productivity and adapting to change. This would take time; the impact of these reforms could be measured not over the course of a few hundred days but over the longer-term economic cycle. The new workplace environment meant that agreements negotiated by unions, which commonly lasted for two-year periods before being renegotiated, might require restructuring in order to boost productivity.

Under my leadership the AWU enjoyed sustained national membership growth. The union's relationships with employers and other unions improved markedly. Our membership was more seriously engaged. We recruited talented young organisers and experts, including women. Towards the end of my time as the union's leader, enterprise agreements at various workplaces were into their fifth round of negotiations. Agreements would typically involve annual pay rises of 4 per cent—sometimes as much as 6 per cent. When you calculate the sum total of those increases over a ten to thirteen year period and add on superannuation contributions and other benefits, it is undeniable that the union I led lifted the living standards of thousands of Australian workers and their families.

For Labor, a strong safety net for Australian workers, including a decent minimum wage, is non-negotiable. The argument that a strong minimum wage causes unemployment just doesn't stack up. Ever since the Harvester judgement, some have argued the minimum wage is too high and acts as a handbrake on jobs and growth. As Massachusetts Institute of Technology (MIT) Professor Joshua Angrist insists, however, the 'burden of proof' has shifted. We know that the minimum wage does not have a large adverse effect on employment levels. On 3 May 2014 Britain's conservative *The Economist*, which had opposed a minimum wage for Britain, issued something of an apology, concluding: 'No-one who has studied the effects of Britain's minimum wage now thinks it has raised unemployment. Partly as a result of this experiment on our homestead *The Economist* has changed its mind.' Theirs is not a change of heart; it is a change of mind based on evidence, not ideology. For Labor, the minimum wage is more than an essential strand of the social safety net—it is a driver of growth. It is vital not only to individuals and working families, but benefits the entire economy, underpinning consumption and further stimulating demand for goods and services, and creating more jobs. Again, this is not a particularly radical idea. In April 2016, David Cameron's Tory government legislated for Britain's first National Living Wage for all employees aged over 25.

The same goes for job security. We must not allow the creation of a vast army of Australians employed in insecure work through labour hire and ever-increasing casual contracts. Working people are not simply commodities who sell their labour and should never be treated as such. We cannot allow the distinction between the weekend and the working week to be obliterated. We cannot allow the destruction of our national tradition of a 'fair day's pay for a fair day's work' through the dismantling of penalty rates, the means by which millions of families put food on the table, which would foster greater social division. It offends against our great national achievement of prosperity with fairness. This is why I have announced new workplace policies designed to protect Australian workers from being ripped off by dodgy employers. A Labor government I lead will introduce stronger penalties for employers who underpay their workers; bigger penalties for sham contracting; the fair work ombudsman will be given increased powers to pursue companies that fall into liquidation and fail to pay workers entitlements; and we will provide far greater statutory protections for overseas workers to prevent their being underpaid and exploited.

Workplace relations are not set in stone in this country. As technology advances, the economy shifts course and social norms change, so too must our approach to wages and conditions alter. It is why my Labor Opposition, through the efforts of Shadow Assistant Treasurer Andrew Leigh, has developed policy principles to guide our approach to the sharing economy so that we have a market that operates in the interests of both workers and consumers. If there's a roadblock confronting productivity, Labor won't be frightened of addressing it. But a dog-eat-dog workplace won't benefit the majority of Australians.

This is another important element of my approach to the workplace: I don't assume that employers are ogres. One of the first pieces of advice that Bill Kelty gave me during his time as ACTU secretary was this: class warriors could destroy one of the great agents for improving the lives of working people—the good employer. The good employer invests in the long-term security of a company for the long-term welfare of employees. The good employer pays decent wages, provides a safe working environment and continuity of work, and offers opportunities for training and development essential to the improvement of workforce skills. If a good employer looks for increased productivity to ensure that working people get a fair share of the profits that result from improved productivity, why seek to frustrate them? If a union weakens good employers, workers are worse off.

Employers are as vital as the workforce when it comes to building the common good. This was the basis of my dealings with all employers. Having decent relationships with employers helped me to understand how businesses go about producing wealth. Because the AWU had breadth across the economy and because my relationships extended into every industry, I understand how things operate at the enterprise level. I know what costs drive business, how input-cost changes affect profit margins, how to deal with operating and capital expenditure, why leverage is so important to businesses, and just how hardworking many bosses are. You can't expect to be prime minister without understanding business. Yet I never forgot what my job was as a unionist and what that would sometimes require. Strength meant being willing to negotiate enterprise agreements that adapted to new circumstances in the workplace.

When workplace laws were reformed in 1993, the life of a union official became more complex. Enterprise bargaining ended the old system of centralised wage-fixing and award pay rises based on entire industries. The new system was dependent on a larger range of instruments: minimum wage rate adjustments, enterprise bargaining agreements and legislated superannuation. The union had to negotiate often complex agreements with employers. If the companies had to be more efficient, so did our union. We had to modernise and professionalise our operations. To improve our bargaining capacity we had to be more businesslike, more democratic and more adaptive. Enterprise bargaining also placed more of an onus on employees to be involved in the negotiating process. In these circumstances, if the employees required training and external advice it was only reasonable that employers should contribute. Under the Whitlam, Fraser, Hawke and Keating governments, the Trade Union Training Authority ran programs to teach workers how to represent fellow employees. Shortly after taking office in 1996, the Howard government abolished the authority, meaning employers had to foot the bill. In the end, it was in the interests of employers that their employees knew how to bargain constructively, which is why some contributed money to the union for precisely that purpose.

These changes, continuing structural shifts in the economy, and the lingering effects of the early 1990s recession coincided with a bad period for the AWU. When I joined the union it was at a very low point. The old AWU, based on a diverse range of rural and semi-skilled or unskilled workers across many labour-intensive industries, had recently amalgamated with a fellow blue-collar union, the Federated Ironworkers Association. The politics and culture of the old AWU were substantially different from those of the FIA. Each had led the good fight against communist infiltration of moderate unions, but the FIA was less centralised and arguably much more modern. The AWU, with the exception of its Queensland branch run at the time by Bill Ludwig, was factionally riven and deeply troubled. Many employers were withdrawing their support and encouragement. Rival unions were circling, preparing to poach its members in the event of collapse. At no stage in its long history had the AWU been at such a low—effectively bankrupt in some states and hopelessly behind in affiliation fees to the ACTU and other bodies. It was internally divided and on the most important test of all—how it was looking after its members—it was failing. Members were paid some of the lowest wage rates in Australia because of years of inactivity.

I set out to reform the union's enterprise bargaining negotiation framework, established building delegates' forums, increased unionist education, refinanced the union and made it clear to other unions that the AWU would work with them cooperatively. I wanted us in the mainstream. I wanted us looking after the basics: substantially increasing minimum rates; enhancing the health and safety of workers; and signing up and organising an expanding membership. I wasn't afraid to look for input from unorthodox places. To that end I had the environmentalist Tim Flannery, Indigenous activist Pat Dodson, Federal Sex Discrimination Commissioner Pru Goward and social demographer Bernard Salt speak to delegates at our modernised national conference. I also wanted to confront the dead hand of factionalism. If I could find effective union officials from other parts of the movement, I was keen to get them working for the AWU. I brought in Dick Gray, a tough operator who came from the Electrical Trades Union, a militant left-wing union; and Helmut Gries, a former Hoechst petrochemical plant worker who had served as shop steward for the Amalgamated Metal Workers Union. It wasn't attachment to the right or the left that mattered to me. Shopfloor experience is always important, but I was prepared to recruit experts and talented go-getters from outside, people like my friend and successor as AWU national secretary, Paul Howes, and others, such as Troy Spence, Kevin Midson, Steve Price and Zoe Angus. Above all, I was looking for commitment, hard work and results.

An important lesson that I have carried from my time as a union organiser into my role as federal Labor leader is the value of empowering people and team-building. I applied them to the workplace and to Parliament, based on the belief that we should start with a simple principle: acknowledge and listen to each other. Listening involves a degree of mutual trust. Organisations with flatter hierarchies that allow people to manage their own tasks are more productive and better at problem solving. You get more engagement and more alignment between employees and organisational goals. You can't do that in everything—an army platoon requires a hierarchy and a court needs a judge. In my experience, however—informed in part by the Jesuit belief that problems are best solved at the most immediate, local level—organisations work better if people on the frontline have more of a say. Ninety-nine per cent of companies I dealt with were interested in bettering safety. And when you examine the health and safety records of companies, it is those with fully functioning health and safety representative systems that are safer. Health and safety is a classic example of empowerment. I have seen employees who know from the slightest sound of a machine that it wasn't running smoothly. Underground miners have told me they can hear when rocks are about to burst—they call it 'popping'. The benefits of shopfloor knowledge apply just as much in the modern economy, especially in tech companies. The music-streaming company Spotify is split into several large groups called Tribes. Each Tribe is responsible for a set of related features or engineering functions. While the whole company works on the core product of Spotify, each tribe is organised to work as independently as possible. This organisation helps remove decision-making bottlenecks and inspires creativity. The point is that when you devolve authority and empower employees you actually get better outcomes.

In the days immediately after the Longford gas explosion, AWU occupational safety expert Yossi Berger and I interviewed two of the contractors who had been working on the giant cylinder that exploded. It had been leaking heavier-than-air gas all morning. There were two supervisors and two operators on shift. Between them they possessed nearly a hundred years of experience. There were two contractors working on the job as well. The cylinder was icing up and all morning they had been trying to fix it. The two contractors left a minute or so after midday. They went to a brick change room about 400 metres away and were shrugging off their overalls when the place exploded. Two of the men still working on the cylinder were killed the other two were badly burnt. The contractors suffered terrible survivor guilt. This was a massive blast. If you look at the security footage, there were nine rolling explosions that resembled Armageddon. We said to these workers, 'How did you know to leave?' and one said, 'My arse was twitching.' The point is: people know. When we're talking about empowering people, instinct can keep people alive.

During my time at the AWU I grew to admire works councils, the committees that can be formed to represent all employees at an enterprise. In Germany, the works council model is mandated by law and is especially popular. It has been an important factor in making that nation's economy dynamic, strong and efficient. It is supported by both sides of politics, along with co-determination, whereby employees are allowed to play a role in the management of the companies they work for, especially large organisations. A conservative Christian Democratic government introduced the latter policy in the early 1950s. Some union officials don't like works councils because they have the potential to challenge the authority and power of unions. I found them appealing: they draw on the irreplaceable, shopfloor knowledge of a company's workforce and promote cooperation between employees and managers. Another reason that some union officials aren't enamoured of works councils is that in the eyes of some they make unions akin to a third party in workplace relations, in addition to employees and employers. I have never subscribed to that view and I didn't see the AWU as a third player when I was involved with the union. When I appeared before the royal commission into trade unions in July 2015, I was startled to find that the commission seemingly adhered to this old-fashioned, third-party view. The counsel assisting the royal commission appeared to question me on the assumption that there was the union here, the employees there and the company over there, and that workers were somehow cheated if the company dealt with the union.

I always viewed my union as merely the expression of the will of the workforce. This is why I diverge from the opinion of some more heavily ideological unions, who say that an enterprise agreement can't be accepted until it fits exactly with every clause in a union's log of claims. I always believed that, as a union official, you push for the best possible option and if the workers are happy and in your own conscience you believe it's a reasonable deal ... well, that's called bargaining. Some workers wanted to go on strike when I didn't think they should. You can explain to them that it would be a mistake. Ultimately, however, you've got to be guided by them. Effective representation means prioritising responsiveness and dialogue.

Some people think strong leadership means telling people what they must do or being the smartest person in the room. That's wasn't my view as a unionist, and nor is it my view now as Labor leader. Real leadership shows that consensus and negotiation is a sign of strength, not weakness. Real leadership means understanding the minimum and the maximum that people will accept. You go for the maximum, yet always understand the minimum. In every negotiation I have been involved in, I refer to the 90:10 rule—let's work on the 90 per cent we agree on, not the 10 per cent where we differ. This is the belief I have carried into politics.

3

A CHANGING WORLD

MOST AUSTRALIANS ARE optimists. We know our country can fashion a great future for itself . We are blessed with smart people. We possess the ingenuity, resilience and work ethic to create and maximise new opportunities. Egalitarianism is part of our collective DNA—we have the enduring values to keep our society cohesive and fair.

At the same time, many of us are worried about the future. The Australians I speak to are anxious about their jobs and covering their mortgages; security in retirement and supporting not just their kids but their parents too; and protecting themselves and their families from exposure to illicit drugs, violence and terrorism, as well as the darker side of the web. We want to know how our kids will cope in a rapidly changing world and who will care for our parents. Australians are asking where the new economic growth will come from; where the new jobs will come from; how we will maintain our standard of living and strong safety net; and how the Commonwealth's budget can be kept sustainable.

Australia is now into its twenty-fifth year of uninterrupted economic growth. There are people aged 43 who have not seen a recession in their adult lives. There is an entire generation of young Australians for whom the distress and disruption of the early 1990s recession is ancient history, not lived memory. Yet inequality is at a seventy-five-year high. I don't believe I've seen the level of concern—the sense of unease— among Australians that I see now. They don't need to read the papers to see that wages growth is at the lowest levels since the early 1990s. Living standards have fallen consistently under the current Liberal government. The number of unemployed and underemployed people continues to be higher than at any point during the previous Labor government. Stockmarket volatility is greater than usual. Australians are concerned about the health of the global economy, especially China's prospects.

> *The goal of full employment will be at the core of the policy agenda of the national government that I lead.*

Some of these trends are out of our control, but unsatisfactory leadership hasn't helped. There is plenty of talk about there being a plan, but no plan has been put forward, which only adds to the unease already being felt by Australians as they seek to adapt to big changes in their daily lives, with no guidance, encouragement or basic understanding from our national government. Instead, the prime minister jokes that he is leading the country on some *Thelma and Louise*–style road trip with his sidekick Barnaby Joyce. And we all know how that movie ends.

All modern politicians must confront our world's seismic economic and technological changes. Since I started work, factories that employed thousands of people have been flattened or converted into apartments. Manufacturing jobs that gave people straight out of high school predictable, stable and reasonable incomes have been erased from the landscape. Our steel industry is at a dangerous tipping point. Service industry jobs have been undermined by increasing casualisation, automation and contracting. The haemorrhaging of manufacturing jobs needs to stop, as does the attrition of crucial job skills. We should be a shipbuilding nation and in the business of building submarines, too. It's in our economic and national security interest. We are an island nation, after all.

Too many Australians are at risk of being left behind. I've seen what happens when a person doesn't have a job—the loss of income, increased family pressures, rising anxiety, a lack of hope, the loss of a sense of identity and the inability to plan ahead. Unemployment also corrodes people's relationships with others. If you have a job, you've got a stake in society. People without a job for a long period can give up on the idea of working altogether. This is happening in today's Australia and wreaks havoc socially and economically—impacting on the daily life of families, workforces and communities.

Younger Australians, especially, are experiencing changes to the nature of their jobs and income, the blurring of the line between work and recreation, and changes to their relationships and expectations of what a good life entails. Because of the Coalition government, young people are being hit with increases in university fees and face seeing their penalty rates stripped away while support for job-seekers and apprentices is slashed. Their superannuation is being undermined and the government is prioritising the interests of speculators ahead of young first-home buyers. The Australians who will build the next age of our nation's prosperity deserve so much better.

It's no good trying to pretend that we can stop still or turn back the clock on all of these changes. The only option for political leaders is to understand what's happening and to take responsibility for helping Australians adapt to these changes. This is not a time for government-by-slogan or excitable rhetoric. Australians understand that unlike previous generations, they won't have a job for life. In our suburbs, regional cities and country towns, people want to know if they and ultimately their kids are going to be OK. What jobs will they be doing? Will they be able to afford a home of their own? What do they have to do to acquire a well-paid, purposeful job and keep it? What sort of skills do young people specifically require? They want to live a meaningful life outside of work. They want to be able to smooth their prosperity over their lives and to maintain their health and that of their loved ones. Most know that lifelong education will be a common part of their existence—because the premium placed on higher skills will only continue to grow. They want to be able to keep up with the rapid pace of change in our world, to be able to cope with what the American poet Robert Frost once called 'the shafts of fate'—a sudden illness, an ageing parent to care for, divorce, or a brother or sister who urgently needs your help.

These concerns sharpen as time marches on. As I write, I'm 48 and increasingly mindful of how age shifts our perspective. It seems to me that as people reach their mid-forties they start thinking about things they didn't worry about at age 20 or 30:

long-term financial security; mid-life health; and how their quality of life will change as they move towards retirement. In my union days, whenever I held meetings to talk about claims for extra superannuation and enterprise bargaining, workforce opinion was generally divided by an almost a perfect dividing line—the age of 43. Of course, the workplaces were mainly male and blue-collar. Under age 43, super wasn't a big drama. After 43, everyone paid attention, not unexpectedly given that this is half the present average life expectancy of Australians.

Australians are wondering whether they will have enough money to survive on in the future. Once upon a time Australians had a simple 'hump' in their wealth acquisition. You had kids in your twenties and thirties, and by your forties you were trying to pay down your mortgage. Nowadays, it's almost like you have two humps, first in your twenties because you put off having kids and you have some disposable income. Then you hit your thirties and forties, and it's the hard slog through raising kids and a mortgage. The second hump now occurs in our fifties, when Australians return to accruing income and savings and want to smooth things out because, from this point on, that money has got to last until their eighties. This is a trend that is changing the way we live. The key to understanding this trend is the changing nature of work itself. A generation or two ago, many young Australians simply chose a version of what their parents did for a living. But many of the jobs that we will be doing in fifteen years have yet to be invented. Australians are confronted by both a jobs challenge and a jobs opportunity. I think we're ready.

What jobs our kids will do in the future is a global barbecue stopper. The World Bank and the International Labour

Organisation have each pointed out that the world's largest economies are struggling to generate enough jobs. This is a long-term challenge. Gallup, the American research group, speaks of 'the coming jobs war' in which there will be five billion people over 15 years old in the world, three billion of whom will be hungry for work. Yet there will be only 1.2 billion full-time, formal jobs to go round. We're talking about a reorientation of the global economy. The competition for skills and resources will be fierce.

The overarching global challenge is to expand the pool of decent jobs in the face of productivity increases derived through automation and digital developments. During the first Industrial Revolution and its aftermath, advances in productivity led to more jobs. The new digital revolution does not appear, at this stage, to be following the same pattern. What MIT economist Jared Bernstein terms the 'Jaws of the Snake' phenomenon has seen productivity growth and employment growth diverge since the end of the 1990s. Likewise, productivity increases have not led to commensurate wage growth. If they have, wage growth has tended to flow to the top 20 per cent of the population.

This 'decoupling' of productivity and growth is likely to prefigure significant changes to our economy over coming decades. It signals a major shift in income from labour to capital, changing business models and increasing use of technology to replace human involvement in producing goods and services. The digitisation of services—a combination of increased computing power and mass data—will reshape our perceptions of employment, including those occupations that we previously considered to be highly skilled. These changes underline two important priorities for governments across the world: first, the focus must be on employment, not just growth; and second, that the most important response to these changes is empowering labour forces through education, training and upskilling.

That's why the goal of full employment will be at the core of the policy agenda of the national government that I lead. There are longstanding arguments over what full employment really means, but when it comes to jobs and the economy, our goal should be making sure everyone who can work is able to work to their full capacity. We should never be completely satisfied with an economy in which hundreds of thousands of Australians are unemployed, and many more are under-employed. Moreover, the objective of full employment has to be underpinned by decent wages and a strong safety net: it is a goal that means little unless it improves living standards and household incomes.

Part of the jobs challenge means understanding other unprecedented changes taking place in our world. For a start, automation, digital connectivity and complex global supply chains have changed how we work in the space of just two decades. Developments such as quantum computing, nano-technology and 3D printers will no doubt continue to revolutionise work and production processes in the years ahead. Every new development broadens the canvas for the next development. We know that technological disruption is likely to create jobs in new industries—think of coding and robotics—and new ways in industries where we are doing old things, such as healthcare and education. Yet in many existing businesses, disruption is likely to replace more jobs than it creates, as robotics and analytics allow companies like Australia Post, Telstra and Woolworths do more business with fewer employees.

Our climate is also an important thread in this story of economic change. With the global effort to reduce harmful climate change gathering pace, we have to think hard about ways to meet Australia's energy needs while shrinking our contribution to global emissions. As international demand for carbon-intensive mineral exports falls, we have to seek out new and different trading opportunities. A hotter, drier climate combined with more frequent extreme weather events is also making life difficult for Australians in some of our oldest industries, notably agriculture. All of these changes force us to re-assess how Australian industries work, and what place each has in our economy of the future.

At the same time, our population is ageing. This shifts the balance between those in the workforce—and contributing to growth—and those outside of it, contributing to our community in others ways while themselves needing services and support. Thirty years ago there were 7.3 people of working age for every Australian over 64; today that number has fallen to 4.5 people. The latest Intergenerational Report projects that by 2055 this will have halved again to just 2.7 working people for every older Australian. Our ability to ensure a dignified retirement for older Australians while keeping the budget sustainable is going to depend on keeping the economy growing strongly, especially as we face the headwinds I have just mentioned. We will, however, have a superannuation pool of $4 trillion. In 2025, 27 million people will live in Australia: 5 million of us will be aged over 65; another 5 million will be aged between 15 and 24. A woman aged 60 in 2025 will expect to live for another thirty years; a man can expect to live for another 27 years. Ponder those statistics and their implications: living until your late eighties and mid-nineties as a matter of course.

We also need to be able to adapt to the big changes that will accompany the rise of Asia. After World War II, Australia opened itself up to trade with Asia by looking at the region in a new way. The first step was rethinking where we stood in relation to our neighbours: the 'Far East' became the 'Near North'. A mental shift was followed by tangible policy change. Australia opened itself up to mass migration, offering opportunities to people from every faith, culture and tradition. We undertook, over time, a shift in the national mindset, transforming our idea of ourselves from a British outpost perched fearfully on the southern edge of Asia to engaged partners in the economic and strategic security of our region. None of this was without risk, and nor was it universally popular. The journey is not at an end. In the 1980s we opened ourselves up to the world again. In the second decade of the Asian Century we stand as the world's twelfth biggest economy, having weathered the storm of the global financial crisis (GFC). Situated in the heart of the world's fastest growing region, we are uniquely positioned to seize the opportunities of this moment—if our country is well governed.

China is not the be-all and end-all of the Asian Century. China, India, Indonesia, Japan, South Korea, Malaysia and Thailand have a combined population of around 3.1 billion people. That's nearly half the world's population. Those seven nations account for around a quarter of the global economy.

By 2050, they will produce 45 per cent of global GDP. By 2030, Asia's middle class will have increased from half a billion people to 3.2 billion. Those 3.2 billion men, women and children will create unprecedented demand for quality services—from health to education to finance to tourism—and unprecedented demand for quality products and produce. The Asian Century is the biggest opportunity since the gold rush of the 1850s. But we're going to have to bend our backs. We will need to plan hard and work hard to ensure that all Australians prosper, not just a few. The Asian Century will create enormous opportunities for the higher education sector only if we strengthen our links with the region, improve our Asian literacy, beginning with more of us speaking the languages of our neighbours, and immerse ourselves in their cultures. Asia is not a dollar sign, or just a market. It's a place of many histories, cultures, religions and languages, which we must learn from. We won't succeed with a 'fly-in, fly-out' mentality towards Asia. Indeed, if elected prime minister, my first overseas visit will be to the Asia–Pacific. Papua New Guinea and East Timor will be my earliest ports of call. My deputy, Tanya Plibersek, has already prioritised our relations with the latter. Under our leadership Australia will be a good global and regional citizen. The good society should not begin and end at our nation's borders.

IN AUSTRALIA WE face specific challenges that make it even more vital that we focus on equipping ourselves to deal with these changes. Australia is at the close of the largest mining investment boom in our history. Mining will continue to be an important industry for a long time to come—yet it does none of us any good to imagine that our nation is seamlessly transitioning into a new economic golden age. The key issue facing Australia today is about how we transition and diversify our economy beyond mining.

Why? Unfortunately, during the mining boom, we allowed our alternative export base to wither. In 2000, less than one-third of Australia's exports came from resources. Today more than half our exports are made up of just three commodities—iron ore, coal and gas. Data produced by the International Monetary Fund shows that Australia's exports are now more concentrated than they have been for more than six decades—since the wool boom of the early 1950s fuelled by the Korean War. Our extreme dependence on bulk commodities is almost unique among advanced economies. This is a new development. Before the recent mining boom, Australia's export concentration was broadly in line with those of similar high-income countries. By 2010 our export concentration had soared. Today, our exports are more concentrated than the average of middle-income countries. In fact, a handful of low-income countries, including Nepal, Kenya and Tanzania, are able to claim greater export diversity than Australia.

Our economy is heavily exposed to volatile commodity prices. Australia's nominal gross domestic product (GDP) is delicately placed, rising dramatically in the decade to 2012 and now descending in a sustained slowdown. The Commonwealth budget is hostage to global iron ore markets, with a $10 price shift able to knock $10 billion from forecast revenues. As the growth in mining exports fades, we don't seem to have much left to fill the gap. It's hard to revive manufacturing exports once plants have closed down, skilled workers have left and customer relationships are lost. It is to the current Coalition government's eternal shame that it embarked on an absurd campaign against domestic manufacturing in the early part of its time in office. Most prominently in 2014 there was the spectacle of Joe Hockey goading General Motors to leave Australia, in effect forcing the company to begin a shutdown of its operations. This produced a cascading effect throughout the automotive sector—a sector much larger than just the big car-making companies. As a result, 200 000 workers were left unsure of their employment future. The government offers no large-scale plan for alternative investment in the economy, especially for manufacturing and renewables.

For a decade, we have been operating on the assumption that, once the mining boom passed, low interest rates and a falling Australian dollar would be enough to revive the non-resource sectors. When the Australian economy transitioned in the past, the dollar typically fell and our automatic stabilisers kicked in: resource exports declined and manufacturing came into its own. With a diminished manufacturing sector, how-ever, this transitional effect is muted. That's a real worry. Also in the past, as interest rates fell, construction activity and investment would increase. This is less the case during the present cycle. Australia is emerging from a high-investment, high-cost mining construction boom. Australians have become seriously indebted at a household level; we are more exposed to fluctuations in commodity prices and stuck in a rut of low domestic growth. The conventional wisdom is that services will replace the 'old' economic activity. However, the take-up from this sector seems to be inadequate. Services have started to grow as the dollar has fallen. Other than education and tourism, we haven't yet made the most of these export capacities. This is the case even if we accept projections showing that in ten years health and care services will be our largest employment sector. The Coalition government's diabolical economic and fiscal strategy has badly undermined national confidence. Neither prime minister has fostered the transition in investment necessary to balance out changes in the economy.

My plan for the next generation of Australian prosperity—of rising productivity, growth and jobs—begins with education.

There's no need for despair just yet. Australia possesses one of the highest per-capita income levels in the world. We have sufficient economic capacity to reposition ourselves. Our fundamentals are solid. When Labor was last in government we gained a hard-won AAA credit rating from the three major ratings agencies for the first time ever, giving confidence and certainty to business and investors, and retained it through the storm of the GFC. We must preserve it. Our banks are some of the largest and safest in the world; our legal system and democratic institutions are stable and respected. Our superannuation savings pool is the largest in Asia and the largest per capita in the world. Our education system supports a high-quality, productive workforce. Our cities are, on the whole, wonderful, diverse places to live. And we adapt faster and better than most—for example Australia went from lagging in the smartphone revolution to number two in the world in terms of smartphone penetration in just one year. A good barrier draw doesn't mean the race is won. We have to put our hard-earned advantages to work. When he was treasurer, Paul Keating used to talk about 'pulling the levers' of economic reform. There is no way for modern Labor to simply update and reintroduce the changes implemented in the Hawke/Keating era. You might as well persuade Australians to swap their satnav for a Melways or UBD Gregory's. Australia has changed dramatically in thirty years—socially, economically and technologically—in large part because of Labor's nation-building reforms. Modern Labor seeks government in a different world, a digital age where instead of the traditional levers we engage with the complexity of an economic touchscreen. This means being selective and strategic in where we invest and what we prioritise, getting behind our best natural resource: the work ethic, creativity, brains and resilience of the Australian people.

That's why my plan for the next generation of Australian prosperity—of rising productivity, growth and jobs—begins with education. We must lift education standards across the board, from pre-literacy in childcare, technology in primary and secondary schools, science at university, vocational schooling and re-training for mature-age workers or parents returning to work. It's why Labor, through our recently announced *Your Child, Our Future* policy, committed to funding the Gonski school reforms in full over the next decade. Better education outcomes lead to higher wages. We are a fair-wage nation, in a low-wage region. We don't want to compete against other nations in a race to the bottom. That's why I'm focused on creating even higher-wage, higher-skill jobs, and nurturing and attracting the best minds. I'm passionate about revitalising advanced manufacturing, especially in defence and biotechnology. The paramount ambition of a Labor government has to be creating good jobs, jobs with a future and jobs of the future. The linking up of work and knowledge is the key to Australia's mature industrial economy maintaining its competitive advantages.

The next treasurer of Australia, Chris Bowen, is a generous Labor man. His Christmas gift to me in 2014 was a book written by the MIT Professors Erik Brynjolfsson and Andrew McAfee, *The Second Machine Age*. The authors suggest that information technology and digital communication are reaching the point at which they will fundamentally change the lives of all humanity. Yet they warn of the prospect of these new technologies throwing very large numbers of people out of work. One passage in their book struck a chord with me. It got me thinking about my kids and their future working lives: 'There's never been a better time to be a worker with special skills or the right education, because these people can use technology to create and capture value. There's never been a worse time to be a worker with "ordinary skills" and abilities to offer, because computers, robots and other digital technologies are acquiring these skills and abilities at an extraordinary rate.'

To take another example: look at how fast solar technology is evolving. In the last five years alone, the cost of a solar cell has halved. The cost of battery storage has been halving every eighteen months. Early in 2015 Tesla released its plans to produce a rechargeable lithium-ion battery that consumers can operate at home. Very soon, someone, somewhere, will find a way to make solar power even cheaper and more efficient. You can count on that. I want that someone to be an Australian. I want Australia to own that breakthrough and for all Australians to share its benefits. I want us building,

designing and refining solar technology here. The solar industry already employs more Australians than the coal sector, and
there is no doubt this gap will grow.

Wanting Australia to do well, urging enthusiasm and
excitement, isn't enough. Governments have a role to play in
planning for the future, not just hoping something will turn
up. In fact, I know that Australia already has the skills and
technological capacity to exploit the opportunities offered by
new battery technology. We need only look to the work that the
CSIRO has done in the field to see that. In Melbourne, Nissan
Casting is creating electric componentry for its 'Leaf' model
car, having taken advantage of a $3 million co-investment that
was begun under the previous Labor government. Another
developed nation proves the point. When commentators
speak of the West German 'economic miracle' that began in
1948—and the continuing resilience and dynamism of unified
Germany's social market economy—the label is a misnomer.
Sustained national prosperity didn't occur by accident, but
required cooperation between governments, business and
workforces—the common good in action. Australians know
this too—it was demonstrated by the critical reforms undertaken by the Hawke/Keating governments of the 1980s
and 1990s.

So how do we get there again? Let's consider one of the great
social and human changes taking place right now: longevity.
In coming decades, it will become commonplace for most
Australians to look ahead to a century of life well lived, with up
to half a century of learning and meaningful work. Our future
working lives will be more varied than previous generations
have been used to; it won't mean fifty years of eating the same

lunch at the same desk in the same firm. No one expects one job for life. Fifty years ago, women were not encouraged to pursue a career—and men weren't expected to change careers. Now the average time spent in a job is three years and four months. Already, we average seventeen different employers in a lifetime and at least five separate careers. Those numbers are only going to increase as we further diversify. So even if, at the age of 18, someone chose a law degree over science or arts over commerce, or university over TAFE, those decisions are not final. Future Australians could easily end up doing two or three TAFE courses over a working life and probably return to university—while also completing a range of shorter courses through private providers. During my time as a union official, I decided to return to night school and university by way of completing a Master of Business Administration degree. Multiple careers won't proceed in some neat sequence. There will be overlap and interaction; success in one field might drive someone to another field; a contact met through one industry might inspire a move to a different one, perhaps even overseas.

We will have to become a learning society from early childhood right through to training and re-training in our sixties and seventies. Education is the key to adapting to the big changes underway in our world. It is the means towards unlocking a new era of national prosperity beyond the resources boom by building an economy defined by a diversified industrial base and good jobs. Education is an investment, not just a fiscal outlay. The world-leading economist Joseph Stiglitz makes the same point in his book *Creating a Learning Society*. He argues that there are essentially two types of economic efficiencies: static, which means cutting red tape and taxes;

and dynamic, which is about investing and empowering people, chiefly through education but also through creating new industries for people to work in.

Australians deserve to get ahead because of how hard we work and what we know, not because of who our parents are or the 'postcode' they live in. Australian society is at its best when it is ruled by the laws of meritocracy and we work together for the common good. This creed is the key to our nation's ability to adapt to a changing world and preserving the Australian Way in our lives. It will be the defining ethos of my government.

4

A FAIR GO FOR ALL

ADAPTING TO THE fundamental changes underway in our economy must involve governments, businesses, workforces and the community pulling together. This is the Australian Way, where consensus and fairness go hand in hand with individual aspiration and personal ambition, and where wealth creation is balanced by fair wealth distribution.

It's scandalous that at present we have nearly a million people on the disability pension, over three-quarters of a million people unemployed and around 150 000 people unemployed for longer than twelve months. More than a million Australians regularly record that they're not getting the hours of work that they would like. That is a phenomenal waste—nearly 3 million Australians just not in the system. Our opponents like to blame people for their own predicaments; I prefer to look at the system and ask: why isn't the confidence there to create and maintain jobs? What are we doing to tackle the scourges of disability, discrimination and unemployment?

Disappointingly, Australia lags behind the world. A 2011 report by PricewaterhouseCoopers, *Disability Expectations*, found that Australia ranked twenty-first out of twenty-nine OECD countries in employment rates for people with a disability. Australia is ranked last in the OECD when it comes to the relative poverty risk for people with disability.

My concern for people with disabilities and their place in our society stems, to a substantial extent, from my time as the Parliamentary Secretary for Disabilities and Children's Services. This was my first appointment upon entering Parliament in December 2007 as the federal member for Maribyrnong in Melbourne's north-western suburbs. I was also made responsible for bushfire reconstruction in the aftermath of Victoria's 2009 Black Saturday bushfires. Some observers were surprised when news arrived that the newly elected Prime Minister Kevin Rudd had given me the parliamentary secretary position. Admittedly, I knew little about policy-making in this area, but I'm grateful to Kevin for the choice he made. The job gave me the opportunity of working with the deeply experienced Jenny Macklin, Minister for Families, Community Services and Indigenous Affairs, who has fought hard, her whole life, to empower poor and disadvantaged Australians. It allowed me to see up close the trials and challenges of people with disabilities and their families. After fourteen years as a union representative, I thought I had seen unfair treatment in the workplace. I thought I had witnessed disadvantage and powerlessness, and I had. But nothing could prepare me for the invisible world of disability.

The best way I can explain what I encountered is to put it this way: imagine if we built a city with very high walls. Into that city, we exile hundreds of thousands of our citizens—the half a million Australians with profound and severe disabilities. Behind those walls, we put another half a million Australians—the families and carers who love their precious brothers and sisters, sons and daughters, and mothers and fathers. And imagine if we said to the people of this city of a million people: 'From the day you are born to the day you die—from cradle to grave—you will have, at best, a second-class life.' Imagine telling every person with a disability, their carers and loved ones, that by dint of birth or a cruel twist of fate you will forever be a second-class citizen, that behind these walls you will be more likely to be poor and far less likely to finish school, go to university, get a job or own a home. If we built those walls around other citizens, there would be an uprising. The outcry of voices would produce such a chorus so as to tear down those walls. Yet I discovered an apartheid system of disadvantage when I began my time in Parliament. Over my first few months in the portfolio I met young Australians with lifelong disabilities who were forced to live in aged care homes—people aged in their early twenties with their entire lives ahead of them, living alongside elderly Australians in their final days. These were young people imprisoned, effectively, by a lack of choice, exiled not because of their particular disability or lack of aspiration but by the barriers our community had constructed around them.

I bore witness to the shattered exhaustion of parents barely hanging on. I looked into the eyes of parents wearied by sleepless nights of anxiety wondering who would love and care for their precious son or daughter when they became unable to. I spoke with many mothers whose children had

66

been diagnosed on the autism spectrum, who had been called bad parents by ignorant people, and routinely told to 'control' their child. I remember an event where I stood alongside the mother of two children with Down syndrome. What I heard next utterly shocked me. Another woman casually asked of the mother: 'Why did you have the second?' I saw marriages driven to collapse by the physical, financial and emotional stress of caring for a beautiful child with a disability. Yet I was privileged to meet with thousands of inspirational people with a disability who refused to be defined by their disability—people who were able to work, wanted to work, but who were held back by a system that wouldn't recognise their potential contribution and which only comprehended the cost of things, not a person's innate value. Every time I met one of these steadfast people and heard their story, my determination to do better strengthened. It's easy for politicians to praise carers as saints—that's not enough. I believe that people with disabilities and their families just want the right to a decent life. They taught me a lot. I was fortunate, too, that my wife Chloe, who had previously worked in disability services, gave me the knowledge and the networks to talk to people who understood what was happening.

This was a revolutionary moment for me. There was a great wrong that needed to be righted. At the heart of the National Disability Insurance Scheme (NDIS) is the recognition that disability could affect any of us: the beloved newborn, or a toddler whose developmental goals were falling short of expectations, or the victim of a traumatic car accident. Every family is subject to such possibilities. I had seen enough of how things could go suddenly wrong for others during my years at the AWU. Righting this wrong was an issue to which I decided to bring the skills I had learned as a unionist in order to organise a disempowered, and remarkable, group of people. So we began a journey to create the NDIS, a nation-building reform that will improve the lives of millions of people who experience hard days and difficult nights. We set out to replace a fragmented system that arbitrarily allocated resources to people based on crisis and fatigue with a national scheme supported by a single funding pool. We required a system that understood the disability in question, provided a package of funded support and allowed people to make their own decisions. The new system, rather than seeing a person as a charity recipient, saw them as a citizen whose potential was waiting to be unlocked, which in turn would benefit the whole community. The aim was to give people the option of living independently in supported accommodation and working in their communities, rather than relying on charity. They were to be provided with a tailored level of support for everything from home and vehicle modifications to assistance with household tasks and daily care needs. We asked the Productivity Commission to examine the cost effectiveness, benefits and feasibility of a disability scheme. The commission returned with the view that while such a scheme would be expensive, it could indeed deliver significant economic and social benefits. From that point, the issue became one of national willpower.

The NDIS was not just about giving people with disabilities and their families a chance. It was a major economic reform. The scheme introduced a far more efficient and cost-effective model of service delivery. If you put citizens at the core of service delivery and trust them to take control of the use of resources, you will get a more efficient allocation of resources and ultimately better outcomes. Money goes where it is needed, rather than being absorbed by administration costs.

At the heart of the National Disability Insurance Scheme is the recognition that disability could affect any of us.

It saves money over the long run because you provide services in a market-orientated way. It also promotes innovative service delivery because there is competition among providers. The economic gains go well beyond improved service delivery. Carers can suffer from chronic fatigue. They can lose the opportunity to save money for their own retirement. So providing more support and independence for people with disabilities increases the opportunities for carers to participate in the workforce. That boosts national productivity. An expanded labour force— involving more people with disabilities and their carers—drives growth, increases revenue, stimulates spending and reduces demand on government services and transfer payments.

Hindsight makes it tempting to conclude that the NDIS was inevitable, that it was the product of a magical combination of hard-headed policy logic and the imperative of fairness. In fact, the idea was first raised during the Whitlam era of the 1970s and again at the 2020 summit, arising out of the social policy stream chaired by Tanya Plibersek and Tim Costello. And yet the NDIS wasn't Labor policy until 2009—two years into the life of the Rudd government. The Liberals were luke-warm at best. Good change is not inevitable: it is forged by people of goodwill. Without the spirited, co-ordinated, grass-roots advocacy of community groups, public sector leaders and people with disabilities and their carers, the NDIS would never have made it onto the national radar. These were people with the moral authority that comes from a life spent fighting for what is right. There is a tendency today to say that the great fights have already been fought and that we have reached a relative state of prosperity which means there are no longer crucial arguments to be won. This is mistaken. The NDIS happened because a Labor government believed that finding funding in a time of downgraded budget revenues was a social and economic priority.

The lesson I take from my involvement in the creation of the NDIS is that substantial policy trumps spin every time and great policy tops personality. In this era of media fragmentation and the 24/7 news cycle, advocating big and complex ideas is more difficult—and yet more rewarding—than ever before. Voters will reward a political party that takes them into its trust by arguing the case for practical, achievable, worthwhile change. The NDIS was a relatively expensive, complicated policy. Its realisation shows that people are willing to back bold new ideas if the case is made properly. By acknowledging the complexity and the expense, and engaging in a frank and mature discussion with the electorate, we were able to deliver a comprehensive national solution to a problem first identified by the Whitlam government in the early 1970s. At the 2013 election, the NDIS did not deliver Labor popular acclaim or electoral victory. But what matters is when a young person can find a job, or when a person with disability can get access to the ordinary life that millions of other Australians take for granted. Our nation's great achievements, our monuments, should be when a parent or an elderly carer in their seventies or eighties can be told 'your precious child will be OK'.

This style of thinking underpins other challenges a Shorten Labor government will prioritise. We are undeniably a wealthy nation, among the richest on the planet, yet we have persistent levels of poverty that arguably bring our egalitarian national character into question. Inequality is back on the national agenda—exactly where it should be. Since the GFC rocked the foundations of our economic order in 2008, a host of world leaders from across the political spectrum, and leading figures from industry and academia, have urged a rethink of the relationship between equality and prosperity. The International Monetary Fund, the World Bank, the Bank of England, the OECD, and the Vatican all insist that inclusion is the key to growth. The old 'trickle-down' consensus—that growth comes first and then societies can set about doing something about equality—is crumbling: equality is not a dividend of economic growth, it is a pre-condition.

The great achievement of the last Labor government was that access to opportunity and general prosperity was maintained after the events of late 2008. There was a very real risk of generational unemployment. During the 1990s recession I saw people lose their jobs. Some got them back after a long struggle; many didn't. Families, workplaces and communities were devastated. Only Labor prevented that happening again. Around the world there is another name for the GFC: the Great Recession. We don't use the term in Australia because the actions of the Rudd Labor government, especially those of its Treasurer Wayne Swan, staved off a recession. The practical, targeted response Labor instituted in government prevented the kind of consequences we saw unfold in the United States and Europe—double-digit unemployment, mass foreclosures and a generation of young people out of work. Australia weathered the storm and emerged in better shape than any other nation on earth.

Labor knows how to navigate perilous economic, social and technological seas. Each of the trends that will define our future—the rise of Asia, the upsurge in service industries, digital disruption, the development of a clean-energy economy, the equal treatment of women, and the unprecedented experience of two generations of retirees living at the same time in Australia—are all underpinned by the constant requirement to create economic prosperity with fairness. Too many Australians do not feel a sense of economic security; too many want for secure work; and too many lack access to permanent housing. There is a growing disparity in wage rates and working hours. My colleague Andrew Leigh has shown that between 1975 and 2014, real wages in Australia have risen by only about $7000 for the bottom tenth of income earners, yet rose by $47 000 for the top tenth. Put another way, the top 10 per cent of income earners have received a national pay rise greater than the total pay for the bottom 10 per cent. The richest fifty Australians possess more wealth than the poorest two million. That is simply not right and nor is it sustainable.

This pay gap carries serious practical consequences for every Australian. The OECD estimates that the rise of income inequality has knocked 4.7 percentage points off cumulative growth between 1990 and 2010 on average across OECD countries. This is especially significant when we recall Australia's sluggish economic growth. As recent research from the Melbourne Institute's Household, Income and Labour Dynamics in Australia Survey illustrates, wages and salaries are by far the dominant source of household income in Australia: that means a robust and rising minimum wage is always central to tackling inequality. To that end, in 2015, for the first time, Labor from Opposition put a submission to the Fair Work Commission's annual national wage review in defence of a strong minimum wage, because the minimum wage is an irreplaceable source of consumption. Weakening our minimum wage won't boost our competitiveness or enhance social cohesion. Indeed, the Coalition's eternal dream of a purely market-clearing wage threatens our long-term national prosperity.

A fair minimum wage is only one part of the story. Some policy-makers think it is fashionable to talk tough about bludgers, rorters, frauds, cheats and double-dippers. A rather unsuccessful recent treasurer indulged the rhetoric of 'lifters and leaners'. No one condones the small minority who cheat or bend the rules. Yet it is dishonest and lazy to attack the straw man of a bloated welfare system. Indeed, the word 'welfare' itself is used pejoratively in many parts of our media, and by the Coalition government, as a code word for sloth and waste and undeserved income. This is disappointing not because of the cheap, chest-beating rhetoric masquerading as government policy, or the bullying of people who are often doing it tough— it's that the facts tell a very different tale. Australia already has one of the best-targeted systems of social investment in the world. While there is always room for improvement in the way assistance is targeted, it is important to note that Australia spends less on welfare than almost every other advanced country and our system works reasonably well. When those who earn more in a week than people with disabilities or the unemployed or carers will earn in an entire year rail against welfare, it's hard to take them seriously. The Melbourne Institute's Survey shows that around 50 per cent of people on income support are back in work within a year, and 75 per cent return to work within three years. There is a reason why Labor calls

When those who earn more in a week than people with disabilities or the unemployed or carers will earn in an entire year rail against welfare, it's hard to take them seriously.

welfare a form of social investment. The Australian National University's Professor Peter Whiteford estimates that for every dollar we spend on welfare, we reduce inequality twice as effectively as any other nation. On the flipside, cutting social security payments increases inequality twice as fast. Perhaps unsurprisingly, the National Centre for Social and Economic Modelling found that the least-well-off 20 per cent of households were the hardest hit by the 2014 Budget. And to think that the next year Treasurer Joe Hockey had the gumption to tell the same people to get out there and 'have a go'.

The fight against inequality extends to bridging the gender divide. Australia, along with New Zealand, led the way in equality for women more than a century ago. Australian women were some of the first of their sex to win the right to vote. In 1912, women persuaded Andrew Fisher's Labor government to introduce a maternity allowance, a cash payment of £5 to all mothers, excluding, to our national shame, Aboriginal and Torres Strait Islander peoples. Today, Australia's goal should be nothing less than the equal participation of women in work. This means equal pay for women at work. It is not right that systemically Australian men on average earn 17 per cent more than Australian women. Nor is right that it has been at this level for around two decades. Even worse is the existence of a 'super gap', whereby Australian women on average retire with half as much money as men, simply because men earn more and traditionally haven't spent time out of the workforce to raise kids or care for elderly parents. We need an equal voice for women across our Parliament and in our boardrooms. As the *Gender Equity Insights 2016: Inside Australia's Gender Pay Gap* report found, getting more women on company boards helps to bridge the gender pay gap. It showed that increasing the number of women on boards from zero to equal representation led to a 6.3 percentage point reduction in the gap for full-time management staff and a 2.6 percentage point reduction in the gap for other full-time employees. Major studies from Canada and Norway now prove that gender diversity leads to better company performance, financially and in terms of improved decision-making.

Gender equality needs to extend beyond the boardroom and across the entire workforce. Australian industries that are dominated by women have historically paid lower wages. That's why as Employment Minister I was proud that the previous Labor government supported them by backing and then implementing the outcome of the 2012 Fair Work Commission's *Equal Remuneration Case* for Social and Community Services workers. These workers—of whom 120 000 out of 150 000 are women—have challenging jobs, including helping women and children in refuges, running support centres for people with disability, leading teams of counselling professionals, and managing family support services and emergency housing for the homeless and the mentally ill. The Labor government's efforts will mean that these workers benefit from regular wage rises totalling between 23 and 45 per cent from 1 December 2012 until June 2021. If we are to become a fairer society, we need to better value work in the fastest growing employment sectors of the economy—in healthcare and social assistance—and smash the gendered walls of work.

Gender equality is not just a matter of dollars and cents. Australian men need do their fair share around the home. Governments can't resolve the argument over who will clean the bathroom. Yet we know that men who take paid paternity leave stay more involved in household and childrearing throughout their kids' lives. It's fair that men share more of the domestic load, and it's emotionally rewarding too. Most men of our generation want to be more connected to their children than their dads were to them. Another practical means of helping working women balance their family responsibilities with the demands of a career is by supporting paid parental leave and making provision for better childcare. As the child of a working mother I attended kindergarten at Monash University, which was one of Australia's first workplace-based childcare centres. It was a great place and a big help to Mum. Our nation requires a childcare system that is affordable—it is unfair and unproductive for a parent's wage or salary to be eaten up by fees so that they work just to pay for care. Australians need childcare that is accessible—where families and single parents can get places where they need them. We deserve a childcare system that is properly resourced and staffed. There's nothing more important to parents than who you entrust the welfare of your kids to, and childcare workers should be paid on that basis.

The millions of Australian women and children who endure the nightmare of family violence deserve strong national leadership. The first funding commitment I made as Labor leader was not on education, or defence, or innovation—as important as those areas are. On International Women's Day 2015 I pledged $71.6 million for tackling family violence—a down payment, if you like, to pay for important frontline services like legal representation. I have announced that, if Labor is elected, we will provide for five days' paid family violence leave in the National Employment Standards. Women affected by family violence should be able to take leave to access legal and financial advice, counselling services and medical appointments. Survivors and their families should not have the added stress of missing work, or experience the financial uncertainty and added anxiety that creates. Violence against women has many causes and we need to work harder to eliminate them. However, a precondition for women leaving violent relationships is economic security and independence—that means decent jobs, good pay and a strong safety net in tough times. Only in a society where men and women are treated equally across all aspects of their lives can the true potential of all be realised and injustice banished from our national landscape.

I said at the outset of this book that your political position is, in part, defined by the institutions, standards and people you decide to protect. I can think of no public policy debate that encapsulates this belief better—and the imperative of preserving our nation's 'fair go' ethos—than that of universal healthcare. Medicare is a thirty-year-old national institution built by modern Labor, despite the persistent campaign by the conservative side of politics and other vested interests to undermine it. Medicare embodies the Australian Way. Medicare is a community gold standard. If you have nagging asthma, if your child has a rising fever or if your elderly mother is crook—and you're worried it's something more serious—you and your loved ones can visit a GP. It doesn't matter if you have lost a job or you're flat broke. And Medicare works. Our universal health system is smart, modern and efficient—it makes us healthier and more productive because we take less sick days from work. Australians have come to treasure Medicare. It is envied around the world. Because of Medicare, Australia spends barely half as much on health compared to the United States, as a proportion of our GDP. That's less money, for better care, longer life expectancy and greater access. All of this at no cost to employers and no extra burden on business, as is the case in the United States, where companies often pay for their employees' health insurance. It beggars belief that the enemies of Medicare seem intent, once more, on destroying our system of universal healthcare. We saw it at play in the 2014 Budget when the Abbott government sought to introduce a GP tax that would have effectively killed off Medicare's universality. We fought the GP tax and defeated it, at least for now. We will continue to fight against any suggestion that Medicare be privatised. We will fight the government's removal of the bulk-billing incentive for pathology and radiology services, which would in effect create a new GP tax—the latest stealth attack on Medicare's universality.

Like Medicare, healthcare is a threshold test of our commitment to the good society. It reflects the duty a government owes to care for its citizens, and the responsibility we have to be men and women for others. Our health system determines our ability to succeed as a modern, productive, wealth-creating economy. When our children are healthy, they can go to school and learn. When we are healthy, we can go to work and grow the economy. When elderly Australians are healthy, they can enjoy the fulfilling retirement they have earned. In a lot of important ways, we have a world-class health system in this country: one the best-trained health workforces of any nation; the standards of treatment we receive for emergencies and serious illness are among best in the world; our major hospitals employ the latest technology; and we lead the world in advancing new treatments, such as kidney transplants. Yet none of us would or should claim our system is perfect.

There are significant trends we cannot ignore and structural challenges we must address. At present, we have a health system that is focused on treating Australians who are already very sick. We need a system that focuses on keeping Australians healthy. Only 2 cents in every dollar Australia spends on health goes towards prevention. Our hospitals are crowded with people suffering from diseases that could have been treated earlier and managed better. We need to invest more resources in integrated primary care, in prevention, in helping Australians stay healthy—not just managing their sickness. These principles will be at the heart of a Labor government's plan to modernise our health system. The alternative is the Liberals' cutting of $57 billion from the public hospital system and its short-sighted removal of vital procedures from the Medical Benefits Schedule.

Labor's plans begin with a clear understanding and acknowledgement of the health challenges confronting the Australia of 2016. Consider an example that my colleague Catherine King often refers to. A nursing home resident was admitted to an emergency department suffering from ovarian cancer. She was unconscious, did not have an advanced care plan and the hospital was unable to contact her family, so the doctors operated on her. She then spent several days in intensive care, before she died. When the family was reached they said that she was in the advanced stages of dementia. They were unhappy she had undergone surgery, which they believed inflicted unnecessary stress. The hospital doctors did not know any of this. They did their job, like the professionals they are. Yet if they had better access to information, the outcome for the patient and her family might have been better. Consider the contrast. At a practice in western Sydney, in partnership with Medicare Local, drawing on their data to tailor services to their community, the GPs expanded their practice to include an exercise physiologist and a diabetes educator, because of the high numbers of residents in the area with diabetes. The GPs at this clinic now run regular diabetes workshops and a number of their patients started a walking group together. The GPs in this practice spend one morning a week with a parents' group, teaching them about nutrition and exercise for children under five. This kind of common-sense, community-based healthcare is occurring around Australia, often driven by the expertise of our GPs. It's applicable to a range of health policy concerns, including the scourge of obesity.

Chloe sat me down to watch the documentary *Fed Up*. It contained an iconic image of a CT scan showing what sugar does to your brain compared with what cocaine does to your brain; this altered my view on the causes and consequences of childhood obesity. Talking plainly about childhood obesity is not a matter of moralising or theorising or playing the blame game. I have battled with my weight periodically since my teenage years. And now as a father of three I'm acutely aware of the risks our modern diet pose on the health of all of our kids. It's not quite a matter of needing a PhD to decipher the true dietary details of the day-to-day food and drink we consume. But as parents Chloe and I know that reading the fine print on the food labelling of all the products we buy off the supermarket shelf really matters when it comes to our kids' health.

Today in Australia around one in four children is overweight or obese and has a 20–50 per cent higher risk of being obese as an adult, increasing their risk of serious disease. The number of overweight children in Australia has doubled in recent years. This rise is a challenge for all of us, not just because of the health problems it causes but also because of the social problems it leads to, such as bullying. For many years, we assumed that childhood obesity was simply a function of not enough exercise. But the organisation Active Healthy Kids Australia, an innovative collaboration between universities and research organisations, found that while Australia has relatively high levels of participation in sport for children, exercise alone is not sufficient to prevent childhood obesity. Educating parents is one of the keys to avoiding childhood and adult obesity. School programs can help too by encouraging healthy eating habits in three ways: providing healthy food during school time; teaching children to adopt healthy attitudes to cooking and food;

and providing knowledge about healthier eating choices. In some schools children are required to bring fresh fruit for specific 'fruit breaks'. As part of the Let's Move! initiative launched by Michelle Obama, 'Let's Move Salad Bars to Schools' program encourages schools to provide salad bars. This has been shown to increase children's acceptance of eating fruit and vegetables and to develop healthier lifestyles.

Labor wants to encourage better integration, and deeper co-operation, right across the health system to meet the challenges of chronic and complex diseases, and the fact that Australians are all living longer. Presently, too many public hospital beds are occupied by sick Australians with conditions that were preventable—and sadly are now incurable. Too many scarce taxpayer dollars are spent managing and treating late-stage diseases. The cost burden is largely falling onto our public hospitals. This is where primary care and prevention is so important. Healthcare experts estimate that early intervention could eliminate the need for at least 600 000 public hospital admissions each year—that's 600 000 Australians who should get the primary care they need to avoid a stay in hospital and all the stress, expense and inconvenience it brings. This is the economic and medical benefit of investing in primary care. Better preventative healthcare is deeply personal for me. Both of my parents smoked too much for too long. I simply won't accept the argument of big tobacco and its apologists that Labor's proposal to increase the price of a pack of cigarettes to $40 over the next four years by lifting the tobacco excise is a 'tax on the working class'. In fact, smoking-related diseases are the cancer of the working class. Every bit of scientific evidence proves that smoking shortens our life expectancy—each year tobacco kills more than 15 000 people, and its health and economic costs are estimated to run to $31.5 billion—as my parents and too many other Australians and their families have tragically discovered.

The front line troops of our primary care system are general practitioners. I am deeply concerned that GPs are expressing dissatisfaction with the growing demands made on them by their chosen profession. The pressure to charge patients only what will be repaid by Medicare encourages shorter patient consultation times, leaving both doctor and patient dissatisfied. As we know, the attempt by the current government to have doctors collect a co-payment on behalf of the government, followed by a reduction in the Medicare rebate for a standard consultation, produced a major backlash. A four-year freeze on Medicare payments has only added to the sense of dissatisfaction. Recent surveys suggest that only 13 per cent of young doctors contemplating vocational training are considering careers as GPs. Although our GPs are specialists in family medicine, the remuneration available to them is significantly less than that available to most other healthcare specialists. Real healthcare reform must entail attracting more doctors to primary care and providing them with the infrastructure to achieve better outcomes for their patients.

EVERY AUSTRALIAN DESERVES dignity and security in retirement. Australians who work hard their whole lives should be able to retire in comfort and security. In 1996, the neuroscientist and philanthropist David J Mahoney gave a great speech to graduating students at Rutgers University. He said their generation would 'routinely' live to 100, and challenged them to start planning for an 'active fourth quarter', between the ages of 75 and 100. He suggested that the first three-quarters of our lives will be shaped by our engagement in the learning society: engaging, educating, re-training and re-skilling. The active fourth quarter will be defined by the decisions we make today. Australia needs to constantly strive towards fostering a culture that encourages people to save for their retirement. It is why Labor is unshakeably committed to lifting the superannuation contribution rate to 12 per cent. The Liberals have never really been committed to compulsory superannuation. They have frozen the increase in compulsory superannuation not once or twice but three times, and they have increased superannuation taxes on workers who earn less than $37 000 a year. A typical 25-year-old employee will be around $100 000 worse off when they retire because of these changes. As a whole, these decisions will punch a $150 billion hole in our national savings over the next decade.

On top of this, the Liberals, working with the support of the Greens Party, have undermined our retirement income system through their changes to the pension. Together, they effectively put in place an incentive to draw down on assets in the short term so you can claim the full pension over the long term. With half of all retirees set to be affected by these changes in the next ten years, this perverse pension policy will place massive pressure on our retirement income system. By contrast, when Labor formulates retirement policy, unlike the Liberals and Greens Party, we look beyond the headlines and cheap politics. That's the clear principle behind Labor's policy to tighten excessively generous tax concessions given to very wealthy superannuation account holders. This measure will alone return $9 billion to the budget bottom line over the next decade. Based on average long-term rates of return, it will affect only those with more than $1.5 million in their superannuation account. The measure is sustainable; it is fair; and it is fiscally responsible. The cost to the budget of superannuation tax concessions will soon exceed the cost of the aged pension. Federal government inaction would simply equate to an act of economic vandalism.

For a similar reason, I don't support increasing or extending the GST. The regressive impact of this tax will fall on people with lower incomes. Whether it's increasing the rate or broadening the base, the outcome is the same: Australia's lowest-income households will bear the brunt. The most well-off families in Australia spend around 75 per cent of their income. Low-income families, falling deeper into debt, consume 125 per cent of theirs. A far greater share of their family budget goes toward essentials such as fresh food and healthcare. Real taxation reform involves changing behaviour, encouraging growth and productivity, and creating jobs, and more goods and more services. A consumption tax doesn't change behaviour. It won't drive growth. Here is another reason not to increase the GST: countries with especially high forms of indirect taxation are not performing well.

I'm interested in reform that works for all Australians. Our system is presently bell-shaped. If you have no money, you pay no tax—that's little consolation, because you aren't making any money. Australians in the middle of the income range pay a lot of tax and they don't have the capital means to avail themselves of all of the concessions that are available. By contrast, those earning the most money can unfairly minimise their tax exposure. The policy focus needs to shift to establishing a system where all Australians get relatively equal access to tax concessions. Fifty-five Australians who earned over $1 million in a year paid zero income tax in 2012–13. And why should one person be able to claim half a million dollars in tax concessions yet a person on the average wage is able to claim almost nothing? The same goes for superannuation: why should people with millions of dollars be able to receive an unlimited tax concession on their income earned from super while those who have very small superannuation accounts have to pay income tax on their earnings? Why should housing tax concessions deny Australians the opportunity to buy their first home when others are able to negatively gear their seventh property? If fairness and real incentives to attain greater productivity are key national goals—and they're certainly mine—the current concession system needs to be reined in. It is for that reason that a Labor government I lead will also lower the excessive capital gains tax discount to 25 per cent. You can't have reform when only some people benefit. That's not the Australian Way.

I'm interested in other forms of tax reform, too. Today, more small businesses are becoming companies, with the legal protection afforded by limited liability. Incorporation helps promote asset protection, retaining profits for working capital, access to capital gains tax discounts, succession planning and income distribution. Currently, a series of very complicated structures is used to achieve these outcomes. Setting up these structures takes time and money—and maintaining them is even more expensive and even more time-consuming. How can we preserve the ongoing benefits of incorporation without the ongoing burden of red tape? How can we create a single, simplified structure, tailored to small business? One option, adopted with success in the United States, is to create a specific class of corporations for small business. In the case of S-corporations the company itself is not taxed and taxation is worked out on an individual income basis. Our tax system is different from the United States', yet we do need to consider approaches that recognise that compliance measures should be tailored to match the size of businesses. This is a complex change—Labor is prepared for a discussion with small business, representative organisations, accountants and the legal profession to make these arrangements fairer.

Prosperity without fairness cannot be the means of evaluating our sense of national progress. No Australian should ever be considered disposable. My experience in helping to create the NDIS confirmed this view. My purpose as Labor's leader is to unleash the talents of all Australians and provide renewed opportunity for all wherever they live.

5

CREATING A CLIMATE
OF OPPORTUNITY

Climate change has been a fraught issue for both sides of Australian politics. The message that we humans must change our behaviours can be a difficult, confronting one. That's where leadership comes in: explaining that the opportunities for Australia will far outweigh the costs.

My party has long advocated for a market-based mechanism to abate the dangers of climate change, because we understand the overwhelming scientific consensus. Under my leadership Labor supported the repeal of the carbon tax and proposed instead an emissions trading scheme (ETS). Labor has consistently fought against all of the Coalition government's ill-advised legislation to delay acting on climate change. It's because Labor sees dealing with this challenge as a transformative opportunity for Australia, opening up the possibility of using our skills, knowledge and manufacturing capacity to create new industries and fields of learning. Labor has approached each of the 2007, 2010 and 2013 federal elections with a consistent policy of putting a price on carbon. The Coalition, by contrast, supported emissions trading in 2007, before back-flipping in 2010 to oppose putting a price on carbon pollution. In 2013 they compounded their folly by supporting a system that paid millions of dollars of taxpayers' money to major polluters to 'do the right thing'. Under Tony Abbott and Malcolm Turnbull, the Coalition no longer takes climate change seriously. Under Abbott they sought to stoke fear and uncertainty. Nothing has changed with the new prime minister: Abbott's fiscally reckless, ineffective 'Direct Action' swindle remains in place.

Labor's climate change policy has not been perfect. In office, we didn't pay enough attention to the need to tie our endeavours to international action. There was too much explanation of the mechanism and not enough about the why and what Australians would gain. In 2010, we should have called an election on our ETS policy, which could have produced a decisive outcome on the issue. Instead, we decided to implement a fixed carbon price. Yet we were right to support a cap on pollution and implement a market-based pricing mechanism. It will be shown that we were on the right side of history in having real, practical climate change action as a governing priority. We were correct to establish the Climate Change Authority, the Clean Energy Finance Corporation (CEFC), the Clean Energy Regulator and the Australian Renewable Energy Agency (ARENA), and to increase the renewable energy target of 20 per cent based on expert advice and to provide investment certainty.

Before we focus on the solution we must clearly understand the problem we're trying to solve. There is no doubt that our earth is warming; that our oceans and seas are rising; or that humankind is the cause. Each of the last three decades has been warmer on average than any other in modern times, and thirteen of the fourteen hottest years on record have occurred between 2001 and 2015. Last year was the hottest on record, seeing the warmest recorded temperatures since before the last Ice Age. Sea levels have risen by about 20 centimetres on average over the past century, and the rate of increase has been much greater in recent decades. There is no genuine scientific counterargument in the climate change debate. Labor takes climate change seriously, because we take science seriously. Evidence trumps rhetoric every time. Accepting the analysis of the vast bulk of scientists, and acting on it through consistent policy measures, is the sensible thing for any leader to do.

We have a fragile atmosphere, which we all share and which we rely on for our food, our water, our air and our energy. If we do not act, the consequences will be severe. It is predicted we will endure more droughts, more bushfires, more floods and more storms. We're already seeing ever more extreme weather events. The damage to our coasts, our farmland, our forests and our animal life will be irreversible. There will be no new Great Barrier Reef if it is destroyed by climate change. The displacement of people in submerged islands adjacent to Australia is a real concern: climate change is a clear and present danger to our Pacific neighbours. Rising sea levels, king tides and storm surges are eating away land, roads and seawalls. Brackish waters are creeping into village wells, while sewerage systems are unable to cope with floodwaters, in turn spreading disease.

In 2015 I visited Kiribati and met with their remarkable president, Anote Tong, who for many years was *the* voice for taking action on climate change. For Kiribati, climate change is an existential threat. Many of their islands and atolls are less than 2 metres above sea level. I had read this in briefings, but until you see the damage for yourself you can't fully comprehend how urgent it is for all of us to work together to tackle climate change. I have seen paradise drowning. The Pacific Islands will be first affected, but no country is immune.

Doing nothing on climate change carries an economic cost today and in five, ten and fifteen years, not just in fifty years' time. It is irresponsible for political leaders to argue otherwise—to delay the inevitable. We will see longer droughts in parts of Australia, broken by more damaging floods. Forest firefighters tell of growing fuel loads caused by climate change. They know this will lead to more frequent bushfires. We'll see more severe storms too. Higher temperatures will produce more crop-damaging pests and insects. All of this will inevitably force up food prices. Three-quarters of the land Australia currently uses for viticulture will be unsuitable for such purposes by 2050. We may witness a massive decline in agricultural production, especially in the Murray–Darling Basin. Just a 1.1 metre rise in sea level would cause $226 billion damage to our coastal properties and infrastructure. It will jeopardise $5.7 billion worth of tourism dollars sourced from the Great Barrier Reef and lead to the loss of 65 000 jobs in regional towns. An increase in drought frequency will cost our economy $7.3 billion a year—slashing a full percentage point from the GDP.

Widespread shortages of urban water supply are also predicted. Heatwaves have killed more Australians than any other natural disaster, and deaths are projected to double over the next forty years. Rising health costs are projected to run into the hundreds of millions of dollars as we address increased heat-related deaths, airborne diseases, and respiratory and cardiac conditions. In June 2015 the respected medical journal *Lancet* declared climate change a 'medical emergency'. It warned that if we don't act, we will undermine all the progress made in public health over the past half century. This is the practical cost of human inaction.

Think about the economic opportunity cost too. Many nations are taking action today to limit pollution and modernise their economies through clean energy. A

The decisions that we make in the final years of this decade for climate action will have an irrevocable impact on the quality of life of future generations.

high–emissions intensive economy is reckless over the long-run. Australia is the thirteenth largest emitter of greenhouse gases, and our pollution per person is among the highest in the world. As more nations take action on climate change, it will not be long before a lack of climate policy in Australia is an obstacle to trade deals. It is possible that trade negotiations will mandate an effective price on carbon, or border tax adjustments will be applied to ensure a level trading field.

When I met with Al Gore last year he described clean technology and renewable energy as 'the biggest business opportunity in the history of business'. Australia risks missing out. In 2014, clean energy investment grew in China

(32 per cent), the United States (8 per cent), Japan (12 per cent), Germany (3 per cent) and the UK (3 per cent). At the same time, renewables investment dropped by 35 per cent in Australia. In fact, investment in large-scale renewable energy actually fell 88 per cent—from over $2 billion to around $240 million. In the last two years more than 2 million renewable energy jobs were added to the global economy; in the same period Australia lost 2600 jobs in that industry. We were the only advanced economy to go backwards in that time. Moreover, the race for investment and jobs in renewable energy is no longer one between developed economies. Low establishment and exit costs will only escalate the global pursuit of skilled workforces; the competition for investment dollars can only intensify. The longer we delay climate change action, the more expensive it becomes. We can rebuild cities every century, or deal with flood and fire damage in various regions every fifty years. We can help farmers battling drought once a decade. However, if droughts are occurring every year, if extreme weather events transpire every decade, the costs are too great for govern-ment to manage. That's the framework in which Australians will increasingly discuss the climate change challenge. It will be a debate about environmental, economic and social prob-lems, not just the particulars of a market-based or fixed price mechanism based on a market-based solution or even a fixed price on carbon pollution.

Australians do not want to enter the history books as the generation that ignored the perils of climate change or as the generation that surrendered to the selfish clamour of vested interests. Australia can do its fair share. We don't want to leave the next generation with the hard work of transition, with little left over in the 'carbon budget'—the finite amount of greenhouse gases we can emit to limit global temperature rises to 2 degrees Celsius. Time is of the essence in dealing with climate change. The decisions that we make in the final years of this decade for climate action will have an irrevocable impact on the quality of life of future generations.

The Coalition's Direct Action policy does not work. Labor will not continue to subsidise windfalls for companies that are already acting to cut their emissions or needlessly pay companies who pollute to stop polluting. We will honour contracts that the government has entered into, but the largesse ends there. Billions of taxpayer dollars will be saved by killing the policy. We won't leave Australian workers behind—our policies are drawn from the finest of Labor traditions, combining economic efficiency with our zeal for fairness. Labor will secure the goal of decarbonising the economy, while ensuring that our emissions-intensive, trade-exposed industries remain globally competitive. We will pursue a nuanced, sectoral approach that recognises the urgency of taking action but acknowledges the unique context and circumstances faced by some industries and regions. It's how a smart and fair climate policy should work and has worked in leading economies, such as California's.

Our climate change policy is not simply about doing away with Direct Action. It will involve placing a cap on pollution through legal controls on large polluters to reduce their pollution levels and an internationally linked ETS. Our policy will be firmly focused on supporting jobs in strategic industries. We will also reduce pollution through new vehicle emissions standards and promoting the take-up of electric vehicles. We'll protect our biggest carbon sinks and place limits on large-scale land clearing, which increases pollution levels.

At the core of Labor's climate change agenda is a plan to create Australian jobs and lift investment. To do this we need to join rather than be a spectator in the global race for clean technology. The CEFC and ARENA are critical players on our team—or at least they should be. Remarkably, both institutions are on the Coalition government's chopping block. By contrast, we will commission an expert-led Electricity Modernisation Review to ensure that the energy market meets the needs of today's consumers. Labor will double Australia's energy productivity by 2030 by lifting efficiency and cutting costs. We'll put in place a Clean Power Plan that includes a market mechanism for the reduction of high-emission power sources, especially brown coal–fired generation. Labor's plan will support relevant workers and their communities through that process and will make provision for remediation and structural assistance for regions.

At the core of our climate action policy will be renewable energy. Around the world, there are well over 160 nations that have a form of renewable energy targets. Are we prepared to watch the rest of the world make the transition to new energy sector technologies while we are left behind with an over-reliance on fossil fuels? There will continue to be a need for fossil fuels—we can't make steel and cement otherwise—yet we can't afford to ignore one of the biggest business opportunities in world history of investing in renewable technology. As the decades pass, fossil fuel extraction is occurring in more challenging locations, such as deep beneath the ocean or from coal seams and shale beds. Not surprisingly, this process has become more and more expensive.

If we don't modernise our energy system we are putting our international competitiveness at risk. Just as large-scale renewable costs have declined dramatically, household renewable energy technology has followed. Globally, Bloomberg is estimating a $3.7 trillion expansion of solar until 2040. Nearly 60 cents in every one of those dollars will flow through to rooftop solar—more than $2 trillion. We're talking about a seismic shift in the energy mix of developed and developing countries. Recognising the power of technological advances is crucial—between 2000 and 2015 the amount of energy generated by solar energy increased sixty-five-fold.

Australia possesses some of the best renewable assets in the world. We enjoy more sunlight than any other continent and experience some of the windiest weather on earth. We have enough renewable energy resources to power our country 500 times over. Labor's policy of ensuring that, by 2030, 50 per cent of Australia's electricity should come from renewable energy and our long-term target of net zero pollution by 2050 is not about leading the world—it's about keeping up. China is making massive investments in renewables. India is pursuing a 'saffron revolution' in solar. I want Australia to get our fair share of the $2.5 trillion investment in renewables estimated for the Asia-Pacific region by 2030. At the start of this century, experts predicted that worldwide wind capacity would reach 30 gigawatts by 2010. They were wrong. By 2010, that number was exceeded by a factor of six; by the end of 2014, a factor of twelve. At the same time, it was thought that the solar energy market would grow by 1 gigawatt a year to 2010.

In 2015, this figure was exceeded fifty-fold. In 1976 the cost of solar cells was $79.40 a watt. In 2014, it was 69 cents a watt. Between 2010 and 2015, solar photovoltaic prices fell by 75 per cent, and wind power costs by 14 per cent. The cost of battery storage is plunging. By 2020, solar will be the cheapest form of electricity generation in many parts of the world. The trend is unstoppable. An earlier technological advance is an excellent predictor of what we can expect. In 1980 AT&T planned to produce 900 000 mobile phones, as expensive, massive and clunky as they then were, over the following two decades. It ended up making 109 million units. Now there are more than 7 billion mobile phones in the world. We underestimate the potential for future technological progress at our peril. Australia should start putting in place policy settings to capitalise on that unprecedented opportunity.

For the first time, new global investment in renewables exceeds new investment in traditional sources. Australia can be a clean energy superpower. We can be one of the biggest and best markets in the world for this new technology. We can't rely on the free market alone—there is a constructive role for government to play: ensuring sensible and long term–oriented policies, sending the right signals to markets and investors, and demonstrating leadership. Our goals will be to provide certainty and confidence for investors, encourage research and development in relevant institutions, foster effective regulatory frameworks and embolden industries to thrive by generating their own power.

This global movement is being driven by consumers. The operating costs of solar power are decreasing at a remarkable speed. More than 15 000 Australian small businesses have already taken up small-scale solar, taking control of their energy bills. More than 1.4 million Australian families have embraced household solar power—one in three houses in Queensland and one in five houses in New South Wales. Bloomberg estimates that within five years a 4 kilowatt rooftop set of solar panels with a 5 kilowatt hour battery will give you cheaper electricity than off the grid. This is a consumer revolution, as much as it is an energy transformation. It puts control back in the hands of the user, shifting the balance away from the big power companies. Australia today has more than 1 million self-generators—mums and dads, small businesses and local councils. Solar benefits will continue to multiply, as more efficient battery storage and smart-meter technology become more prevalent. Renewable energy is not just about the environment. It's not just about a more competitive price environment for consumers. It's about jobs. Twenty-thousand Australians work in our renewable industry. This will at least double by 2030, with more jobs in advanced manufacturing, installation, maintenance and in programming and development. This is the case for renewable energy: new investment, new industries and new jobs.

In the past, at the Kyoto and Copenhagen climate summits, extremists from both sides of the debate have created excuses not to act. We have seen it on the floor of our own Parliament—when in 2009 the Greens Party teamed up with the Coalition to destroy the first iteration of our ETS policy. For more than thirty years, the very best science has been on the side of climate action. Perhaps too many of us assumed that this would be enough and that the case would make itself. That's not how the world works: reform is not inevitable and progress is never guaranteed. It takes courage and leadership. That's the impression I got when I attended the Paris Summit in December 2015. I met with the foreign minister of the Marshall Islands, Tony de Brum, a wise, determined man, now in his seventies, who has long fought the good fight in the interests of his nation. As a child in the 1940s he witnessed Castle Bravo, the largest-ever nuclear weapon test carried out at Bikini Atoll in the Marshall Islands. As he progressed through to adulthood, he negotiated with US officials over the damage that testing had caused, and then saw the island of Anebok disappear under water due to climate change. Despite hailing from one of the smallest nations, he won enough support from the so-called High Ambition Coalition to ensure that a commitment to pursuing efforts at limiting global warming to 1.5 degrees was incorporated into the Paris Agreement. While this was happening in Paris, in our own Parliament Foreign Minister Julie Bishop made the extraordinary remark that Anebok remained a 'beautiful and accessible beach getaway'.

If we don't modernise our energy system we are putting our international competitiveness at risk.

The investment markets saw Paris differently. Money had been flowing towards renewables before the Paris Summit; afterwards it became a torrent—in Standard & Poor's estimate, more than $16 trillion was invested in renewable energy and clean technologies. For the first time, nearly every country in the world is committed to targets that aim to hold increases in the global average temperature to well below 2 degrees Celsius above pre-industrial levels, with a further commitment to pursue efforts to limit increases to 1.5 degrees Celsius. A further outcome of the Paris Summit that has attracted less attention in Australia was the International Solar Alliance (ISA). Led by India and France, the ISA will fund projects in the sun-drenched countries of the world's tropics with the goal of making solar power more prevalent and more affordable. Why is this significant? Because it involves rolling out real-time technology that will increase our renewable energy capacity. It's being pushed by India and France, who at Copenhagen in 2009 advocated respectively for coal and nuclear. The world is moving on. Only Labor has the practical energy policies to exploit this boom.

In government, Labor's climate policy achieved strong results. In the two years after we put a price on pollution in 2012, emissions in the energy sector—the main industry covered by the carbon price—dropped by 10.4 per cent. After we introduced the renewable energy target, $18 billion flowed into Australia's renewable energy sector. Wind power generation tripled under Labor. The number of jobs in the renewable energy sector tripled. And the number of Australian households with rooftop solar panels increased from less than 7500 to almost 1.2 million. If we are strategic and smart, Australia can power our future prosperity with solar, wind, geothermal and tidal energy. It means Australian researchers, scientists and investors leading innovation and creating economic growth by developing new energy technology and boosting energy efficiency. This is precisely what the CEFC and ARENA are helping to achieve. The CEFC is a productive and profitable enterprise, generating genuine value for taxpayer money. By leveraging private sector investment in low emission technology, the CEFC helps Australian startups capitalise and commercialise ideas. In 2015, every dollar the CEFC invested generated $1.80 of private sector investment. ARENA provides funding for institutions like the University of New South Wales' School of Photovoltaic and Renewable Energy Engineering, which has, for the past three decades, set multiple world records for silicon solar cell efficiency. The Climate Change Authority has been doing its job well, providing authoritative, transparent information and policy advice—in the same way as the Productivity Commission and the Reserve Bank have. The Coalition's policy is to abolish the CEFC and ARENA. Recently the government announced that the CSIRO's climate monitoring and modelling units would suffer severe job losses over the next two years, which sums up all that is wrong with the Coalition's muddleheaded policy-settings. This is to say nothing of its other actions in office: abolishing a price on pollution, undermining the Renewable Energy Target (RET) scheme and making cuts to a range of climate change adaptation programs. There is nothing innovative about these policies.

Some of the biggest policy issues take many years to resolve. For example, Gough Whitlam's Labor Opposition took a proposal for universal healthcare to the 1972 federal election and won, attracting more than 49 per cent of the primary vote. Doctors opposed the policy. The Liberal and Country parties fought against it tooth and nail in Parliament. In 1974, Whitlam called a double dissolution election. Labor won and was able to pass its Medibank legislation at the subsequent joint sitting of both houses. Between 1975 and 1983 the Fraser government could not reconcile itself to this policy settlement and effectively dismantled Medibank. Labor under Bob Hawke won back office in 1983, promising to implement an improved version of its original scheme, renamed Medicare. The result is that more than thirty years later Australia boasts one of the most robust, enduring and widely supported health systems in the developed world, despite the Coalition's continuing ambivalence.

I'm convinced that Labor will be able to introduce, implement and bed down an emissions trading scheme when it takes office. That's because Labor sees climate change action as part of a comprehensive set of policies aimed at renewing and modernising the Australian economy and its workforce. Concern over dealing with climate change is not confined to an inner-city, white-collar elite: it is a blue-collar issue too. Australians should not be tricked by threats of 'they will take away your job'. Australians are not daunted by the future. They understand that doing nothing is not an option and that, once action is taken to reduce carbon pollution, the workforce and the community will be able to use other resources, such as water, far more efficiently. Those involved in heavy industry and trade-exposed industries understand this too. They know that they will get the benefits from new investment once a decisive, committed climate policy is implemented. Whatever challenges are thrown at Australia, there is sufficient resilience and intelligence in our households, businesses and workplaces to look afresh at an issue. After a decade's debate, it's time the nation resolved its position on climate change and got on with the business of making the most of the opportunities that careful, considered, practical action will provide for our people.

6

DEVELOPING A SMART NATION

I T IS THE duty of every government to look well beyond the next election and tailor its policies accordingly. The policy-making horizon should stretch out at least as far as fifteen to twenty years. That's how families and businesses think. If you borrow to buy a home or extend your business, fifteen to twenty years is around the time you would like to be able to pay down your debt. If you have children, you want to be able to equip them for the transition from childhood to adolescence to adulthood according to a similar timeframe. Getting things right is vital—having the ideas and building a consensus today that will set us up for tomorrow and fifteen years on. That's why so many of Labor's goals are aimed at 2030.

Preparing Australia for the modern world's challenges requires modern thinking. The future will be about lifelong education and technology. It will be about embracing and accepting science. Whether we recognise it or not, science already pervades every aspect of our lives, every industry, every activity. Scientists and engineers made the mining boom possible, from the geologists who found and tested the natural resources for their value, to the creators of the machines that dug the minerals out of the ground and refined them. When you take to the road, it's not just the science inside your modern car, with its onboard computer and GPS, that makes your trip comfortable and safe, it's also the road you're travelling on, the surface of which is the result of considerable research. The science of manufacture and design is everywhere—from entertainment to the clothes you wear.

In the future, science will underwrite jobs in health, education, construction, information and communications technology, mining and agriculture. In many cases those jobs are yet to be invented. If you doubt that, think back twenty years to 1996. How many of us had sent an email, scrolled a web page, or used a mobile phone or electronic banking? Think about how our lives and our economy are being transformed by these everyday features. This type of thinking is central to Labor's plan for the future, whether it concerns the economy, job creation, research and development, climate, education, healthcare or technology. It must be about knowledge in all its forms. Manufacturing in Australia has a future and it needs good policy to create newer, advanced industries. Should Australia lead the world in design using 3D printing? Physical manufacturing, which Australia does so well, especially at the advanced stage, uses a different set of skills. 3D printing, however, uses the skills many highly experienced, knowledgeable Australians already possess. In many instances it's just a case of presenting these technological developments to Australians—3D printing, solar energy, wind power—and they will respond enthusiastically.

3D printing is the promise of the Second Machine Age. This vastly more efficient form of manufacturing connects the physical and the virtual, and allows for greater customisation, flexibility and specialisation. We can compete with low-cost countries because this new technology relies on skills. 3D printing has the potential to revolutionise an aspect of Australian manufacturing, shifting us away from mass production in centralised factories constrained by tools and low-cost labour rates, to a world where production is driven by a more personalised, more flexible form of consumer demand. This will give rise to a massive expansion in the number of small and medium enterprises, 'micro multinationals', who specialise in value-adding. This is already happening in Australia, where we have quietly built a niche in aeronautical 3D printed parts. I have visited facilities all across the country, like Quickstep in Bankstown, New South Wales, which produces composite aircraft parts for the joint strike fighter, and Amaero Engineering in Clayton, Victoria, which created the world's first 3D-printed jet engine. The remarkable thing about Amaero is that, while the 'printers' were built in Germany, it took Australian designers, Australian programmers and Australian engineers to develop the process and write the code that makes those printers work.

In just two terms, President Barack Obama has revitalised the United States' manufacturing sector. One of the initiatives underpinning this reindustrialisation is the America Makes program. America Makes is focused on helping the United States excel at 3D printing. It facilitates collaboration among an extensive network of more than a hundred companies, non-profit organisations, academic institutions and government agencies. America Makes has made the United States' 3D printing industry more globally competitive. Australia can do this too. But only if we can get the policy settings right and we drive collaboration between governments, industry, workers and researchers.

In its 2013 report *Disruptive Technologies: Advances that will Transform Life, Business, and the Global Economy*, the consulting firm McKinsey identified the top twelve disruptive technologies that have the greatest potential to drive substantive economic activity over the next ten years. They are mobile internet; automation of knowledge work; the internet of things; cloud technology; advanced robotics; autonomous and near-autonomous vehicles; energy storage; 3D printing; advanced materials; advanced oil and gas exploration recovery; renewable energy; and next-generation genomics. The report sought to place a dollar amount on the value that these technologies could create, concluding that they had 'the potential to drive direct economic impact on the order of $14 trillion to $33 trillion per year in 2025'. The choice for Australia is pretty clear: do we want to create those technologies at home or just buy them after our competition has already developed them?

We can be a more technologically adept, job-creating, smart nation—not a nation of app downloaders but a nation of app designers. Australians must learn to design, refine and operate the next generation of machines—or we will be replaced by them. This will require unlocking the potential of our education system right from early childhood education through to primary school and secondary school levels, to university and TAFE. Teachers are at the core of Labor's approach. We need better training and support for teachers. We also need to get people entering teaching who have degrees from other courses, science and maths in particular, and make provision for superior upskilling for existing teachers.

Technology-wise, we will work to create startup accelerators and open up the space for new discoveries and breakthroughs. Removing red tape is one path. There is also scope for employee share plans. Cross-fertilisation and deeper collaboration between industry and universities is critical. To an extent it's already happening. In a single week in mid-2015 I visited the Walter and Eliza Hall Institute in Melbourne, where I glimpsed some amazing research into cancer and malaria; Monash University, where I witnessed incredible 3D printing of solar cells; the University of New South Wales, nominated by Al Gore as the best institution in the world in terms of solar energy research, where I saw how they were improving the efficiency of photovoltaic cells, and getting about 40 per cent efficiency, which is an extraordinary result. Australia has not missed the boat—but we do not have a minute to waste either.

Labor has never wavered in its commitment to the power of science, technology and learning.

Science and technology are not small-time or boutique policy areas. When I met with the chancellor of Germany, Angela Merkel, she told me how excited she was to visit NICTA, Australia's Information and Communications Technology Research Centre of Excellence. This is the leader of one of the world's strongest, most innovative economies wanting to learn from us. Yet under the watch of our self-styled 'innovation prime minister', in 2014 NICTA's funding was slashed and it was forced to merge with the CSIRO.

We have the opportunity to become an even more innovative nation by leveraging our financial prowess. Increasing financial market integration, higher-frequency trading and more cross-border partnerships and linkages between operators will mean that the round-the-clock financial markets of 2025 will be defined by capitals in three time zones: the Americas, Europe and Africa, and Asia. Each time zone will effectively sustain three to four financial centres. In our region, Sydney must be one of these financial capitals of Asia. Today, only the Tokyo Stock Exchange has more listed companies. Few can match Australia's financial report card: our major banks are some of the world's largest and safest; our legal system and democratic institutions are stable and respected; our superannuation savings pool is the largest in Asia; and our education system supports a high-quality, productive workforce. We have a culture of financial innovation. Nascent financial technology companies are responding to changing consumer needs. We boast world-leading financial-transaction structures for major projects and advanced blockchain database technology. We must put these hard-earned advantages to work. We could create a virtual innovation exchange right here—think of it as akin to a 'NASDAQ in Asia', drawing on the expertise and skills of our finance sector and linking with universities and highly skilled workers.

SCIENCE AND TECHNOLOGY will remodel our cities, the way we work, learn and farm, unlock future sources of energy and design new forms of communication. Labor has never wavered in its commitment to the power of science, technology and learning as the means to transition Australia from the mining boom and power twenty-first century prosperity. That transformation begins with supporting research and innovation, rather than using the latter term as a rhetorical tactic or an excuse to do nothing. It means respecting scientific research and evidence—especially the work of our hardworking scientists, who dedicate their professional lives to expanding the body of human knowledge. Innovation is essential for all industries—emerging and mature. Labor rejects the false distinction between new and old industries. Australia should be a scientific nation that competes with the rest of the world—and wins—because we share a national commitment to science. Innovation cannot be an exercise in speechifying. As the Business Council of Australia president Catherine Livingstone suggested in *Go8news* in November 2015: 'we seem to have gone from the word innovation being banned to suddenly being compulsory, regardless of context ... if we don't start taking a systems approach we will effectively be deciding how to style the rooms, without having built the house'. Labor couldn't agree more.

Some argue that there is no need to undertake research here. As a relatively small player, Australia should just import technology. That is a short-sighted, dangerous view. Australia must be able to continue to produce brilliant discoveries and technologies on our home turf *and* be in a position to adapt research done overseas. Only countries with a strong research base can effectively import science, build on it and adapt it for their own purposes. That is why Labor has set a national goal for government and the private sector, working with universities, research centres and industry, to dedicate 3 per cent of national GDP to research and development by the end of the next decade. This will boost Australia's investment in research and development from 2.1 per cent to 3 per cent of GDP by 2030.

Our aim is ambitious. As it should be—the jobs of the future and our nation's prosperity deserve no less. Our economic competitors scarcely lack ambition. Sweden, Korea, Japan, Israel, Denmark and Finland—some of the leading technology nations in the world—already devote more than 3 per cent of GDP to research. Getting Australia to this level will require co-operative partnerships between business, industry, universities and research institutes. Government has a role to play through creating the right conditions for investment, sending the right signals and addressing examples of market failure.

Science should never have been shunted away in one government department or viewed as an add-on to a ministerial title. It needs a minister and a government that understand that science is the engine of growth, productivity and job creation across all existing and future industries. Science will be at the centre of the work of the next Labor government. We will pursue a new, co-operative engagement with science, research and innovation sectors. In that spirit, a Labor government that I lead will hold an annual cabinet meeting in co-operation with the Chief Scientist, the Commonwealth Science Council, the Australian Academy of Science and other relevant science sector representatives.

Three in every four of the world's fastest-growing occupations require science, technology, engineering and mathematics (STEM) skills and knowledge. In classrooms today, about 40 per cent of teachers teaching science and maths to Australian students between years 7 and 10 do not possess a tertiary qualification in those disciplines. In our schools, participation in science subjects has fallen to its lowest levels in twenty years. Maths and science literacy has also dropped over the past decade. By contrast, countries in our immediate region continue to improve their results. Labor will work to ensure every school teaches coding and computational thinking. It's about giving the next generation of Australians a whole new mindset and skillset. We will support better training for 25 000 current STEM teachers. In this way teachers will have the confidence to help more students fall in love with science, technology and maths—students who will potentially go on to work and teach in these areas. Labor, if it wins government, will write off the HECS-HELP university debts of 100 000 STEM students—including 50 000 places for women—upon graduation to encourage more Australians, particularly women, to study, work and teach in these fields. At present, the typical science graduate will pay off a $44 000 HECS debt over eight years. Our plan will give the next generation of Australians an incentive to study STEM subjects, and give them a head start in their working life. All Australians will benefit in the long run.

Women make up only 20 per cent of enrolments in engineering and related technologies, and just 14 per cent in information technology. Boosting the representation of women in STEM degrees will be a priority of a Labor government. If women were represented in STEM enrolments in the same proportion to their overall undergraduate numbers,

Australia could double its number of software engineers. As the US National Center for Women and Information Technology recently pointed out: 'Groups with greater diversity solve complex problems better and faster than do homogenous groups, and the presence of women in a group is more likely to increase the collective intelligence of the group.' Fairness is an issue here too. If women are shut out of influential positions in industry and government due to a lack of relevant skills and experience and continuing gender bias in hiring practices, this will perpetuate the gender gap within the Australian IT industry. For instance, in Australia today only one in five tech entrepreneurs is a woman. In her 2015 book *Unfinished Business: Women Men Work Family*, the American thinker Ann-Marie Slaughter reminds us that women surged into the professional workplace decades ago. Yet the ideal worker is still imagined as either a single person or someone with a spouse at home to take care of family matters. Slaughter is adamant that it's workplaces, and not women, that must change. They need to become more flexible places capable of dealing with unpredictable modern lives. We may have to reconsider our conception of what a two-career household and a successful career arc looks like in the future.

Australia excels at discovery. In medical research, for example, we account for 1 per cent of the world's expenditure, yet produce 3 per cent of the world's output. Some of our most significant manufacturers are biotechnology companies, such as CSL and Cochlear. Despite this success, we are second last in the OECD when it comes to research collaboration for small and medium enterprises, and are last in regards to large firms. We need to work together to bridge the divide between what our scientists discover and what our businesses use. We need to stop good ideas, unfulfilled breakthroughs and frustrated innovators falling into a void or heading overseas. To help our businesses harness good ideas a Labor government will create a $500 million Smart Investment Fund, based on the proven success of the former Innovation Investment Fund. We will also work with industry to develop a partial guarantee scheme, StartUp Finance, to arrange microfinancing so that great ideas can get off the drawing board. From Opposition, we have also worked to help facilitate the development of a crowd-sourced equity funding regime for innovators and put in place tax incentives to connect venture capital, angel investors and startups. Let's ensure that the ideas that are born in Australia grow up here and create jobs here.

Australia would not be heading off on some frolic in pursuing these policies, it would simply be keeping pace with advanced countries. In Britain, David Cameron's Conservative government runs the Knowledge Transfer Partnership (KTP) scheme through Innovate UK. This body links individual businesses with a university and a recently qualified graduate to work on a specific project. The graduate, who works at the company, is employed by the university. In turn, the business benefits from the new skills and thinking brought by the graduate. The duration of the three-way partnership is flexible. Depending on the needs of the business and the project's nature, projects can last for as little as six months to as long as three years. The program is part-funded by government grants. In the United States, a similar approach to innovation is regarded as uncontroversial and enjoys bipartisan support. A Labor government will introduce a new body, Innovate Australia, an independent agency that will provide much-needed certainty and strategic direction for business, the academy and the research community. The new body will minimise the risk of political interference and the damaging effect of changes to government innovation policies that occur with each election cycle. It will be staffed with independent experts and business practitioners, selected on the basis of their professional and technical expertise across a range of industries.

Australian startups have a role to play in creating the jobs of today and the jobs of the future. The Australian tech startup sector has the potential to contribute 540 000 new jobs in the next two decades. Australia has some great startups. We pioneered new ways of using technology through companies such as Computershare, Seek and Looksmart. And now newer companies, such as Atlassian, Campaign Monitor and Freelancer, already have a combined market capitalisation of around $3.5 billion. Even newer companies, like Canva, Envato, Aconex and Rokt, are growing rapidly. We need more companies like this. A Labor government will create a Startup Year for final-year or university graduates. By expanding the existing income-contingent loan system (HELP), 2000 young Australians each year will have the opportunity to undertake an additional business-focused year of university (or similar) accelerator or incubator to develop their ideas into a startup business. Universities are the key to driving innovation in other ways. We will need another 100 000 information and communications technology (ICT) workers in Australia in the next six years. To produce those workers, current university course offerings will have to keep up with technological disruption. Three in five university students are being trained in occupations where the vast majority of jobs will be radically affected by automation in the next ten to fifteen years. Among vocational education students, this number rises to 71 per cent. In particular, we need to focus on lifting the low levels of female and mature-aged workers within the ICT workforce. Access to capital is critical. More needs to be done to build stronger links between venture capital and one of the largest savings pools on the planet—Australia's superannuation funds. This is why Labor, if elected to government, will establish an Innovation Investment Partnership, bringing together venture capital, superannuation funds and startup stakeholders. We have started this important work in Opposition and have brought together the key players to begin discussions. Ultimately, the driving force behind everything Labor in office should do in the twenty-first century is to plan for an ever-expanding range of opportunities for our businesses, families, workers, students, researchers and inventors, entrepreneurs and artists—the broad sweep of the population—and foster a smart nation culture that celebrates and promotes calculated risk-taking. The focus of a Labor government should be big picture reform that retools people already in business and work, while better preparing younger Australians for challenges in their adult lives.

THE OPPORTUNITY PROVIDED by education is an Australian right that belongs to us all. Prime Minister Gough Whitlam carved out modern Labor's mission statement in 1974: 'People should be free to choose the kind of education they want, but this choice must be one between systems and courses; not between standards ... Not between a good education and a bad one. Not a choice between an expensive education or a poor one.' We still hold to this belief. Opportunity in education is a pact between generations—a promise to pass on an education system that is better than the one you inherited. For Labor, universities are not just research centres and not just places of teaching; they are the foundation on which to build a better nation. A better education means that Australians are more likely to get a better job and earn more. Education goes beyond mere utility. Education fosters skills, knowledge and resilience—the basis of self-respect and respect for others. A highly educated, skilled workforce is more productive, which benefits us all. Investing in higher levels of education means our children are more likely to be healthier, live longer and engaged in their communities. Education is about discovery, friendship, excitement, fun, a sense of identity and cultural enrichment. Education teaches us how to live and work together to build a better future. That applies whether a student is progressing through early childhood education, school, university or TAFE.

Education is the bedrock of prosperity with fairness. To that end we need to rethink how we approach early childhood education. Many studies now show that kids who are enrolled in early childhood education are better prepared for their future studies and for life outside the classroom. As my colleague Jenny Macklin's important recent social policy report *Growing Together* demonstrated, access to quality childcare and early childhood education is more likely to give Australian children a better start to life, particularly children from vulnerable and disadvantaged families. Quality early childcare, as I suggested in an earlier chapter, also has the potential to bridge the gender gap by empowering more working women and men to lead rewarding careers while attending to their family responsibilities. And as Jenny's report also showed, investing in childcare and early childhood education is not only good for Australian families: quality childcare makes for better, more cohesive communities. It is great for our nation's economy. Research by PricewaterhouseCoopers has estimated that the economic benefit from Australian children receiving a higher quality early education and care program would be up to $10.3 billion (cumulative to 2050), increasing to $13.3 billion with the increased participation of vulnerable children. Labor's plan to invest in better early childhood education will mean that more Australians can achieve their true potential.

The same lesson applies to later learning. A recent OECD report found that for every dollar Australia spends on a university student's education, the average return is five dollars—the second best return of all the OECD nations. That's before we consider that universities provide us with the doctors in our hospitals, the teachers in our classrooms, the lawyers in our courts, the social workers in our community and the countless other occupations that make this country tick. The same OECD report also sounded a note of caution. It identified the strong link between the quality of the education a person received and quality of life—the career they choose, the income they earn, and their overall health and wellbeing. That's why we voted against Christopher Pyne's 2014 university 'reform' bill in the Parliament. Because we believe in equality of opportunity and affordable, accessible higher education for all Australians, we voted against $100 000 university degrees, and the doubling and tripling of university fees. As I told Parliament, we will never consign the next generation of Australians to a debt sentence. This is policy territory that involves and affects potentially every household and family in the nation, not just students. Accessible, affordable education acts as a tremendous agent of social mobility. Yet if university education is available only within the circle of families who have already enjoyed its benefits, it serves only to perpetuate and exacerbate inequality. This is why Labor opposed every incarnation of the Liberal plan for $100 000 degrees—not just because of its unfairness, but because it also weakens our nation's ability to prepare for the future.

In the 1980s and 1990s Bob Hawke, Paul Keating and Education Minister John Dawkins took care to build a sustainable financial future for our higher education system, without imposing inequitable, upfront fees. The Rudd and Gillard governments extended new opportunities to low-income households, and to rural and regional Australia. There are 750 000 students on Australian university campuses today and one out of every four is there because of the previous Labor government. We removed the cap on student places, creating new opportunities for 190 000 Australians. We increased the number of Indigenous students attending universities by 26 per cent. More than 36 000 extra students from low-income families got the chance to go to university because of Labor's reforms. At the University of Western Sydney, sixty-five in every one hundred of its domestic students are the first members of their family to go to university, and one in four of its domestic students come from poor families. One in three of its domestic students speak a language other than English at home. Nearly one in every three of its Australian students are mature-age—Australians re-training and acquiring skills to adapt to the modern world. We boosted funding for regional universities by 56 per cent and we lifted regional student numbers by 30 per cent. We should also never lose sight of the importance of our regional learning institutions. An estimated four of every five graduates from regional university campuses begin work in that region. They provide an immeasurable social return to the communities that supported their education.

More students are studying at university than ever before in Australia, but we need to do more to ensure that all Australians have access to a university education. The next wave of university reforms will have to focus on guaranteeing quality and completion. That means starting university, completing university and getting a good job. The Australian higher education sector should, in the future, offer that as an implicit contract with students. Regrettably, in recent years completion rates have been falling. Growing cohorts of Australians who enrol in university don't graduate. They leave university with a student debt, but no degree. This poses fundamental questions for the future of higher education. How do we ensure and preserve that fundamental principle of accessibility and equity? How do we grow participation rates for students without undermining the quality and value of a degree? For Labor, this is not a matter of forcing down enrolments to improve graduate quality: it is about lifting standards to catch up with new levels of access and equity, and improving student support programs. Governments and universities need to shift the focus from just *enrolment* to *completion.* Equity is not just about getting first-years in the door: it's about making sure our students complete their degree. I have announced that a Labor Government will set an ambitious goal to increase the number of students completing their study by 20 000 graduates per year from 2020. We will work with the university sector to ensure that the demand-driven system has incentives to achieve this goal. Because students need to graduate equipped with the skills, knowledge and resilience needed in their working lives,

Labor's plan to invest in better early childhood education will mean that more Australians can achieve their true potential.

a Labor government will invest an additional $31 million in Tertiary Education Quality Standards Australia, Australia's independent national regulator of higher education. By lifting the quality of teaching and providing better resources we can ensure that students graduate with a high-quality education that will get them a great job. A sustainable funding model is critical to giving the tertiary sector more certainty. Our solution is a student funding guarantee valued at $9000 more per student on average over the next decade, funded by offsetting savings measures. Greater certainty means that graduating students will be more highly skilled, highly adaptable and technology literate. That's good for them and for our economy. We want the best combination of excellence, equity and accessibility to benefit all Australians: that is true for all our higher education institutions—our universities, our TAFE colleges and our private providers.

There are also significant challenges in vocational education that need to be addressed. The sector has the highest dropout rate of any part of our education system, and vocational education and training (VET) qualifications provide a smaller earnings boost than high school or university qualifications. Part of the problem is that dodgy providers have been allowed to run rampant. In the past year the number of Australians taking up an apprenticeship plummeted by 20 per cent. Our vocational system has a proud past, yet it's worth looking overseas for inspiration. Germany's apprenticeship system has a dual system of vocational training and education where apprentices divide their time between work and school. It is a system that produces far higher-quality tradespeople. The United States calls its vocational education a 'two year college', and it facilitates far better pathways between VET and university. Some of the resources that are directed towards assessing 'quality assurance' at our top universities could be usefully shifted into better assessment of vocational training. We cannot create the jobs and industries of the future without a strong TAFE sector, and without training and re-training our workforce. TAFE is essential to creating jobs in our regions, skilling young people, helping mature-age workers adapt, while also modernising our industries. And we have already made it clear we will be backing public TAFE—because the pendulum has swung too far to dodgy private providers of questionable quality. If Labor is elected to government we will undertake a comprehensive National Vocational Education and Training Sector Review to build a superior and more resilient VET sector.

Labor wants an Australia where the opportunity of education belongs to everyone, town and country, man and woman, mature and young, regardless of their postcode or their parents' wealth. The Liberals want to create a country where a university education is a privilege available only to the few.

We want a smart Australia where it doesn't matter if you're born in a housing commission flat or if you live 100 kilometres from the nearest town: you will go to university or TAFE if you work hard. A child's future should be determined by their aspiration and hard work—nothing more and nothing less. We have no option other than to create a more educated, skilled workforce. Two-thirds of all the jobs created in Australia by 2020 will require a diploma qualification or higher. Our economy will need 60 000 new teachers and education assistants; 100 000 new medical professionals and carers to help our ageing population and to oversee the implementation of the NDIS; and engineers, architects and scientists to build the clean energy economy and modernise our cities. Investing in education isn't just about training people to fill vacancies created by our changing economy: it's about preparing our society to anticipate and shape change, not just reacting to it. Education is where the common good is first forged. The price of our minerals will rise and fall but the greatest resources Australians possess are the minds, capacity, potential and the imagination of our people.

7

BUILDING THE NATION

A S PRIME MINISTER I want to be known for my obsession
with full employment—the leader who gets Australians
working, keeps people working, skills people for work and then
makes sure people have the means to support themselves once
they retire. To get there we need to locate and sustain new
sources of economic growth and we need to get the country
moving through infrastructure and actual projects, not empty
promises. As the mining boom has eased, and especially since
the 2013 election, there's been too little Commonwealth
investment and not enough focus on infrastructure planning
and investment.

In its last period in office, Labor had the foresight and
political courage to begin building one of the largest pieces
of innovative, growth-inducing infrastructure in our nation's
history, the National Broadband Network (NBN). This twenty-
first-century Snowy Mountains Scheme will empower more
Australians to work from home and engage with clients and

colleagues online; improve our schools; and boost our international productivity and competitiveness. By contrast, Malcolm Turnbull, as Tony Abbott's communications minister, and now as prime minister, has made the NBN slower and doubled its cost. A prime minister who boasts of his innovation focus has managed to replace tomorrow's fibre network with yesterday's copper. Furthermore, the Liberals have sidelined Infrastructure Australia, the independent body we established to bring more independence and rigour to the assessment of projects.

Australia's infrastructure deficit is an economic challenge that demands strong national leadership. Our nation needs to adopt a generational approach, built on political consensus. At the moment, Australia faces an infrastructure conundrum. We need significant investment in long-term physical assets to underpin our future growth. However, governments at all levels are not able to fund them sufficiently. For example, Infrastructure Australia has estimated that the economic cost of underinvestment in transport infrastructure is projected to reach $53 billion a year by 2031. Yet we have deep reserves of domestic capital in superannuation just waiting for stable and reliable assets to invest funds in over an extended period. Unlocking this capital will be an important contributor to our economic prosperity and help solve our infrastructure conundrum. We must do more to bring major new projects to fruition and to provide support for investment through a consistent, independently assessed, bankable infrastructure pipeline. Currently, state governments are reluctant to bring projects to market because of limited capacity, fiscal constraints and limited funding certainty or support from the Commonwealth. At the same time, very high bid costs, commercial risks, high development and construction costs, forecasting errors, long procurement times and uncertain process have made new infrastructure investments less attractive to long-term equity investors like superannuation funds. The current arrangements are structured poorly—often the interests of constructors, governments and investors are out of alignment. This needs to change.

The Commonwealth must establish processes that foster trust and certainty. We need to ensure that infrastructure projects enhance productivity, are priced efficiently and fairly, are internationally attractive and competitive, and provide a return to the community. Quality infrastructure is central to driving Australia's economic growth, creating jobs and boosting our productive capacity. The right investment in transport, energy, communications and water infrastructure will deliver smarter, more liveable cities—and better-connected regions. This means having a plan for unclogging our roads, addressing outdated and overcrowded rail networks and modernising our energy networks.

My goal is to start the approvals process within the first 100 days of government. Labor will improve the way all infrastructure projects are assessed, structured and selected, to secure a bankable, stable pipeline of long-term work. We will facilitate easier and more transparent bid processes, ensure more certainty and independence in the development of projects and more cooperation in their delivery. Proposals would all be assessed and brokered by Infrastructure Australia. Labor would ensure that Infrastructure Australia is once again a completely independent body, properly funded so it can do its job. Decisions will not be designed to favour Liberal or

Labor electorates; projects on the priority list would have to favour the national interest—from the drawing-board to their physical construction. In order to take the politics out of infrastructure decisions, I commit to consulting with the Coalition on all board appointments.

To drive greater private sector investment Labor will establish a $10 billion financing facility for Infrastructure Australia to provide a combination of guarantees, loans, equity investments or other financial instruments to get new projects underway. This facility will be capitalised with government borrowings, taking advantage of the historically low cost of Australian government debt. It would also help to address the more generous borrowing rates that the Commonwealth enjoys compared with state governments.

Importantly, this financing facility would operate only where there is market failure and where projects are expected to deliver a return on their investment. This will ensure that there is flexibility in financing arrangements to deliver the most efficient and effective arrangements on a project-by-project basis. The financing would be the minimum necessary to get a project up, and then the investment would be moved on to newer projects. Its aim is not to crowd out private sector investment. The CEFC works on the same basis, and every dollar of investment delivers around $2 return for taxpayers.

This new process will also help harness Australia's world-leading expertise in infrastructure development. Macquarie is the largest global infrastructure asset manager; IFM Investors is a global pioneer and leader in infrastructure investing; and Australian construction firms are engaged in projects throughout Asia. When the G20 decided to situate its Global Infrastructure Hub it chose Sydney as its headquarters.

There are tens of thousands of potential jobs awaiting the start of new infrastructure projects. This is to say nothing of the economic benefit derived from more efficient businesses, quicker freight movements, and reduced time for people to get to and from work. More efficient roads mean less pollution. Better public transport connects people and communities, and creates more liveable cities. As a child I used to catch two trains to school and two trains home. It was an exhausting journey after a long day learning and playing. I have heard of Monash University students who live in Melbourne's inner-south who, in order to attend its Clayton campus, are required to travel by tram to the city, then catch a train to Huntingdale station and finally board a further shuttle bus direct to the university. The journey exceeds one hour. This state of affairs was not acceptable in the 1970s and is scarcely so in Australia in 2016.

A Labor government I lead will play a key role in ensuring that a wide range of projects are underway to drive job creation and better transport, working closely with Infrastructure Australia and the states. We welcome the building of an airport rail for Badgerys Creek servicing western Sydney's new airport. Yet Labor has a bigger and bolder plan to revitalise nation-building infrastructure projects. We will build the Melbourne Metro, boosting productivity across the city by reducing the pressure on an overburdened train system. In Queensland, we will prioritise Brisbane's Cross River Rail, increasing transport capacity and easing congestion with a second connection to the CBD. These three projects alone would create over 10 000 jobs in construction. We will also fast-track the Pacific and

Bruce Highway packages, delivering thousands of direct and indirect jobs, and upgrade Tasmania's Midland Highway. Our plans extend to investing in public transport in Perth, a project to improve traffic flows in one Australia's most congested cities, and the Gawler Line electrification in Adelaide. A national government I lead will ensure the Commonwealth funding to get these projects underway and completed as soon as possible. We will work with the private sector to get good projects up and going. Building these projects is Labor's priority—because building infrastructure creates good jobs.

I have been a supporter of very fast and high-speed rail since the late 1990s. High-speed rail technology and infrastructure works. Around the world millions of people use it every day. High-speed rail systems now operate in fourteen countries, and companies based in Japan, China, Korea, France and Germany have experience in constructing and operating successful high-speed rail projects. It would be a game changer for our nation and will revolutionise interstate travel. In government, we commissioned the most detailed study on high-speed which showed, that the economic benefits outweighed the costs. On the Sydney to Melbourne section alone, high-speed rail would return more than two dollars for every dollar invested. High-speed rail has the capacity to turbo-charge the economic potential of regional communities in areas like the Gold Coast in Queensland, Casino, Grafton, Coffs Harbour, Port Macquarie, Taree, Newcastle, the Central Coast, Southern Highlands and Wagga Wagga in New South Wales, Albury-Wodonga on the New South Wales–Victoria border, and Shepparton in Victoria. It's a project that stacks up.

We just need a government with the vision and courage to make it happen.

Substandard infrastructure will cost all Australians. The distance between where we live and where we work is growing fast. Most of the economy's newest jobs are within 10 kilometres of our CBDs. Yet most of our population growth is occurring in our outer suburbs, typically located more than 20 kilometres away. Today, nine out of ten of us spend more than ninety minutes a day travelling to and from work. This poses a fundamental question about our quality of life and our individual lives outside work. Do we want to be a country of three big cities, ringed by drive-in, drive-out suburbs? A nation where parents are never home in time to kick a ball in the backyard, help out with the homework or share a family meal? A country where the next generation of Australians feel shut out of the housing market? By contrast, my vision of a smart twenty-first-century plan for infrastructure means new roads and public transport, new ports and bridges, better social housing, smart energy grids, efficient irrigation projects and, of course, the best digital infrastructure. A coordinated network of infrastructure means that we can unlock the potential of our regional centres to create new growth corridors serviced by rail, road, air and the NBN—in addition to good schools, hospitals and aged-care facilities. This approach would help take the pressure off our cities, and deliver productivity boosts for tourism and agriculture.

The key here is better process and smarter funding. Better processes to develop productivity-enhancing infrastructure have been backed by a host of experts: the International Monetary Fund, the Reserve Bank of Australia, the Business

Council of Australia, AiG, Infrastructure Partners Australia and Morgan Stanley. Inevitably some critics will seek to make this a scare campaign about debt. Others might say that our approach will crowd out private investors. These criticisms are wrong. The current opportunities to borrow and invest money to create wealth in the future should not be ignored. Let's bring on a bigger and better debate about the future of infrastructure and an informed discussion about borrowing to invest in our nation's future. Australian families borrow money all the time, most commonly to buy their own homes. Australians don't take the irrational view that because buying a home means borrowing money from the bank that they will pass over the chance of home ownership in favour of paying rent for the rest of their lives. Before they borrow, Australians do their research and ensure that they pay the right price for their home—a home to serve their family's needs, which will, over time, appreciate in value. We should bring the same mindset to government investment in national infrastructure. Even using a conservative analysis, such as the one prepared by Infrastructure Partners Australia, which assumes no additional leverage, shows that $10 billion of infrastructure investment will directly create approximately 26 000 jobs and add around an extra $7.5 billion every year to Australia's economy.

Quality infrastructure is central to driving Australia's economic growth, creating jobs and boosting our productive capacity.

Nation-building infrastructure projects should be seen as a long-term investment in Australia's productivity and prosperity, and as a short-to-medium term driver of jobs and growth.

Kick-starting infrastructure is critical given the transition underway in our nation's economy. Indeed, building the infrastructure of the twenty-first century is not an optional extra but an essential tool of governments who invest wisely in our national interest.

8

KEEPING AUSTRALIA SAFE

T HE FIRST AND most fundamental task of any national government is keeping its citizens safe. For the modern Labor Party, a strong and robust defence policy has at its heart the principle of self-reliance. Australia, as a free, independent, medium-sized power, seeks to promote a free, independent foreign policy, a policy that promotes a world community that values the rule of law, possesses strong international and regional institutions, and cherishes human rights and free trade. We don't want to live in a world where 'might is right'. Our resolve to promote a rules-based global order must mean that no aspect of our national power serve as an auxiliary for foreign interests or goals. Rather it must be in the service of Australian interests and values. Together with a strong diplomatic posture, engagement with the region and the world, and a generous and targeted foreign aid program, the 'hard power' of our defence capabilities is essential to national power.

I have been interested in matters of defence and national security since my university days. As a young man in the 1980s I watched Kim Beazley and then one of my mentors, Robert Ray, both make their mark as extremely effective and widely respected defence ministers in the Hawke/Keating Labor governments. Around the same time I was motivated to join the Army Reserve at Monash University. I was already a keen student of the history of Australia's military engagements and I was fascinated by the ebbs and flows of the Cold War, a conflict that convinced me of the necessity of our continuing alliance with the United States. This is the first pillar of Labor's vision for Australia's international affairs; the second pillar is closer engagement with the United Nations and other multilateral institutions; and the third pillar, a more comprehensive relationship with the Indo–Pacific region. Upholding these pillars is vital to our defence and national security requirements.

Labor is the natural party of defence and national security. It was Labor politicians who ensured the Royal Australian Navy possessed the capabilities in 1914 to dominate the South Pacific and sweep German colonial power from our own region. At Gallipoli and on the Western Front, it was working people who made up the bulk of the Australian Imperial Forces. It was the great Labor prime minister John Curtin whose leadership guided Australia in the darkest days of World War Two. Curtin stood up to British prime minister Winston Churchill and brought Australian troops back from the Middle East to confront the threat of Imperial Japan in Papua New Guinea and the South Pacific. It was Curtin who established the foundation of our nation's enduring alliance with the United States. It was Curtin's leadership that kept his party and Australia unified as Japanese planes bombed Darwin. He died in July 1945, six weeks before the conflict's conclusion—as one observer put it 'a war victim if ever there was one'. At the outset of the Great War and again during the dark days of World War Two, when Australia's survival as an independent nation was threatened, it was Labor that most clearly understood our nation's defence and national security needs. Labor has always conceived of Australia's middle-power role in the world most clearly. This

> *Labor believes it is appropriate that Australia undertake a significant modernisation of our own Australian Defence Force.*

is why Labor politicians such as Bert Evatt played a key leadership role in the United Nations during the late 1940s, and it was Gough Whitlam's Labor Opposition that pressed for the recognition of Communist China in 1969, some years before US president Richard Nixon went to China at the urging of Henry Kissinger. It is why Labor pressed for Australia's election to the UN Security Council during our last period in office, in the face of vacuous mockery from Tony Abbott's Opposition.

During my time as leader, the government has come to the opposition wanting to talk to us and offering us briefings on national security. It's not always fair dinkum consultation. Sometimes it's a matter of going through the motions. On other occasions, the conversations have been genuine, based on a shared concern about our national security. That is as it should be, from our point of view and from theirs: it's the least the Australian people should expect. I do not see national security as a point of great contention between the parties—the US alliance is vitally important, as is the need to play our

134

part in the security of our region—and I do not think it should be used to create divisions.

Unfortunately today's international system and the rules-based global order we seek to sustain and enhance is under grave stress. This stress can be seen in the Ukraine, in Syria and across the Middle East, on the Korean Peninsula and in the South China Sea. As the economies of the Indo–Pacific countries grow in wealth, the nations of Asia have undertaken to build military modernisation programs of great significance; new submarine, fighter, sensor and missile technologies abound in our region. The primacy of the United States in our region is no longer uncontested. Australia is in a region with neighbours who are increasing military spending. For these reasons, Labor believes it is appropriate that Australia undertake a significant modernisation of our own Australian Defence Force (ADF). While comparatively small, our ADF has always enjoyed a significant capability edge, based on its superior technologies and the professionalism and dedication of its all-volunteer force. To keep that edge, Australia must make the necessary investment in its people and its resources. For a start, that means not insulting our defence force personnel with a real pay cut.

In 2013 Labor originally nominated the target of defence spending as 2 per cent of GDP. As Labor Leader, I recommitted the ALP in Opposition to that same target in 2015. I believe that a credible trajectory towards 2 per cent is capable of bipartisan support and is in Australia's national interest. The ADF must not only modernise its existing capabilities, it also needs to become a more capable, nimble and potent force in the future. Expanding situational awareness, intelligence, and surveillance and targeting systems is a first-order priority. Modernising our maritime capabilities must be a key focus: as an island trading nation, Australia must possess a capable navy. The ADF must also adapt to new and emerging challenges, such as cyber warfare, managing our increasing reliance on technology in space, and countering the growing ballistic missile threats and the proliferation of ever-more capable defence systems throughout the Indo–Pacific. We must foster the innovation and research in both the public and private sectors that can prepare Australia and our defence industry for the security challenges of the near future, such as robotics, autonomous unmanned aerial and underwater systems, laser technology and so much more.

For Labor, the notion of self-reliance in defence policy is important. Self-reliance has disappeared from the 2016 Defence White Paper. That's a big mistake. Labor will bring self-reliance back. We won't surrender the notion that the ADF is an organisation of sovereign capability, capable of independent combat operations to defend Australia and our interests in our immediate region. The ADF must be structured to operate independently in our region, notwithstanding the significant implications this has for the ADF and for the Australian defence industry—a vital partner in maintaining our cutting-edge military capability.

My defence team, of Steve Conroy, David Feeney and Gai Brodtmann, and I believe that a capable and engaged defence industry is a strategic capability in its own right. Industry is a vital enabler of our nation's military capabilities and it also has enormous potential for exports, for jobs, for innovation and other commercial linkages, and even for nation-building in the regions and remote areas of our big country. Labor's commitment to self-reliance has underpinned our resolve to build our future submarines in Australia. The submarine enterprise, established in the 1980s, must continue to build a sovereign capability—submarines that are built, repaired and sustained in Australia.

So too with the major surface ships of the Australian Navy. In 1914 Australia had the shipyards, shipbuilding program and surface ships and submarines it needed to secure our nation and the trade routes that sustained it. The Australian Navy was 'in all respects ready'. It was ready because of the foresight and hard work of Andrew Fisher's pioneering Labor government. When the Opposition Labor Party faced the voters at the September 1914 election the Great War had already begun. Labor was the underdog—the Liberal government was presumed to benefit from incumbency during a time of war. Labor's official election manifesto was called 'Australia Safe'. Labor had good reason to call it that, as Fisher said within its pages: 'The record of the Labor party is the best claim to its fitness to govern during this great crisis'. The electorate trusted Labor and it won a landslide victory. That lesson should be remembered by all Australians today.

Labor knows that we dare not face a serious crisis knowing that Australia does not possess enough vessels, seafarers or engineers to meet the needs of the Australian Navy. Building the next generation of submarines, frigates and destroyers in Australian shipyards is an investment in our national security and our national capacity—a complex and diverse economy, innovation, skilled jobs and technical skills, all vital enablers for our ADF.

Australia's defence policy must necessarily focus on our own region. It is here that our allies and much of the world look for, and indeed expect, Australia to play a key leadership role. Australia is the largest and wealthiest nation in the South Pacific and among the Pacific Island Forum nations. We have important strategic and economic interests here and it is critical that Australia strengthen its relationships with Pacific island countries. We would boast the most Pacific Islands–literate cabinet in years, owing to the

Under my leadership, Labor has consistently sought to build bipartisanship on national security issues. Keeping Australians safe transcends politics.

strong pre-existing engagement from key shadow cabinet colleagues such as Tanya Plibersek, Richard Marles and Michelle Rowland. Our foreign affairs spokeswoman, Tanya Plibersek, has committed a Labor government to repairing Australia's relationship with our newest neighbour, Timor Leste—the cornerstone of which will be the renegotiation of a permanent maritime boundary. We should be concerned about the strains on governance occurring in some Pacific island countries. A number of them confront intensifying threats from transnational crime, poverty, unsustainable population growth, environmental stress (deforestation, exhausted fisheries), and the impact of climate change. These factors mean an increasing need for ADF humanitarian assistance and disaster relief operations, and potential stability operations, like the Regional Assistance Mission to Solomon Islands (RAMSI). It is concerning that Australia's position as the principal security partner of Pacific island countries is no longer guaranteed. This has been highlighted in recent months by China's naval visits to East Timor and the South Pacific, and Fiji's acquisition of Russian arms and equipment.

The priorities of our defence policy should be an enhanced ADF regional presence, increased multinational military exercises, high-profile humanitarian assistance and disaster relief efforts to assist neighbours in distress, and the Pacific Maritime Security Program, which would build on the success of Kim Beazley's Pacific Patrol Boats Program. The Security Program should aim to build a shared maritime domain awareness across the Pacific, to the benefit of combatting transnational crime and the illegal, unreported and unregulated fishing that undermines the security of Pacific island countries. We must achieve greater coordination with New Zealand and France (New Caledonia and French Polynesia) on maritime security and disaster relief.

Looking to the south and Antarctica, the Hawke government played a key leadership role in building the treaty architecture that still governs that continent, protecting its environment and ensuring that Antarctica remains a demilitarised space. The Australian Antarctic Territory covers 42 per cent of the continent. It is incumbent on the federal government to ensure that science and cooperation are preferred to militarisation and armed conflict in this zone. It's so critical to our national interest. To secure that interest, Labor would bring a new focus to the Australian Antarctic Territory. It is absurd that Australia lacks the capability to inspect or even visit the Russian and Chinese research stations built in a part of the world where Australia claims sovereignty. Next to the three Australian stations, our Russian neighbours have built seven stations and China possesses two. The cost to Australia of any breakdown in the Antarctic Treaty would be enormously greater than the cost of us getting this right, right now.

One of the great challenges of our time is the rise of global terrorism. As I write, the people of Brussels have become the latest victims of a wanton act of hate and criminality. Innocent lives were snuffed out through the actions of a barbarous few claiming to act on behalf of Daesh. This organisation and its supporters stand condemned in the eyes of the entire civilised world. Daesh are totalitarian zealots who are beyond redemption. Along with the rest of the world, Australians bore witness to this barbarism last November when terrorists launched a coordinated series of attacks in Paris, murdering 130 people and injuring hundreds more. Tragically we saw its evil at work on our doorstep. In December 2014, Man Monis took hostage employees and customers at the Lindt chocolate café in Sydney's Martin Place, leading to the deaths of two hostages. The current terrorism challenge is unlike any we have witnessed in our history. Lone wolf, low-grade attacks, combined with the sophisticated use of social media and asymmetrical violence, require new thinking. The Labor Party I lead believes that, when it comes to fighting terrorism, we are all in this together. It's important to approach the complex threat of terrorism in a clear-eyed, cool-headed and rational manner. This is not a conflict between states or between nations—it is a transnational threat, and it is a deadly threat in Yemen, Somalia and Nigeria as well as in Iraq and Syria. The same brand of extremism that our men and women are fighting in the Middle East threatens us here in Australia. One message must be made clear—time and time again.

The handful of Australians lured to the war zone in Iraq and Syria, or tempted to replicate acts of terror here at home, do not reflect the values of Islam.

Nor do they represent our nation's diverse and generous Muslim community. I have heard many Muslim leaders say Islam is a religion of peace and I know they mean it. Not for one minute would Labor ever seek to dismiss the threat of terrorism or minimise it. We know there is never any excuse for targeting innocents. Those who seek to cross the very clear boundary of right and wrong should feel the full force of the law. Yet we cannot drain the swamp of terrorism by military means alone. Our goal has to be to work with the Muslim community— through cooperation, not isolation. When thinking about this task I often turn to the advice of the former director-general of ASIO, David Irvine. As he said in his 2014 National Press Club address: 'the strongest defence against violent extremism lies within the Australian Muslim community itself'. This must inform a more balanced approach to counter-terrorism and community engagement. And given Australia's character, history and love of freedom, there should always be a strong presumption in favour of the liberty of individual citizens. What is required is not propaganda, but facts. And rather than hysteria, we need dialogue and practical help for those who keep us safe. Meeting this challenge involves ensuring that our security agencies have all the technical resources and capabilities they need to prevent and defeat threats now and into the future. It means there must be seamless coordination between our agencies and the efficient flow of information. We must ensure that we match the most effective capabilities to a threat in the most timely and appropriate manner that will save lives.

It also involves providing the appropriate resources to foster community engagement, which in the long term will help ensure that these threats do not emerge in the first place.

I have had the privilege of visiting the men and women of the ADF when deployed on operations overseas, in Afghanistan, Iraq and elsewhere. I am always awestruck at their confidence, professionalism, dedication, patriotism, and sense of purpose and mission. All of us are blessed that there are always some in every generation of Australian citizens who make the defence of our nation and its interests their personal responsibility. Australia in the contemporary world still needs such men and women—Australians who practice the profession of arms— and every Australian should be grateful that we possess them.

Over recent decades many Australians have lost much of their former confidence in our institutions, in our banks, our churches and even political parties. There remains one notable exception: Australians place great faith and confidence in our ADF. It is a quintessentially Australian institution and a source of pride and trust. That trust must be cherished and nurtured by the ADF. The ADF must live its values of professionalism, loyalty, integrity, courage, innovation and teamwork. Australians must continue to trust the ADF with their sons and daughters. By necessity, the ADF must reflect the values and diversity of the society it defends.

Every time we send the young men and women of the ADF on operations overseas, we can be confident we send our nation's finest, each of them an ambassador for all of us. It seems that every Anzac Day commemoration attracts ever greater numbers of Australians, young and old. We remember all those who made the ultimate sacrifice, and those who come home forever changed by remorseless war. Like every Australian who has visited Anzac Cove, I was struck by the very steep cliffs and the three ridge lines that confronted our young men so far from home in the chill dawn of 25 April 1915. Australians do not celebrate military glory; we do not seek empire or territorial conquests. We commemorate a legend of free and independent spirits whose discipline derived less from military formalities and customs than from the bonds of mateship and the demands of necessity. On Anzac Day 1943, with war raging in the Pacific, Prime Minister John Curtin paid tribute to our brave armed forces:

> What the men of Anzac did ... was a thing of high courage, of selfless sacrifice, of glowing heroism. To-day the sons of Anzac stand between us and aggression [and they are] called upon to preserve that free life for all of us. Their deeds ... have been potent in their contribution to the cause of civilisation. The Anzacs march again tomorrow. The spirit of free men still breathes. It is an unquenchable spirit. It is a victorious spirit.

The Australian War Memorial was opened in the dark days of World War Two. Curtin called it our national 'treasure house'— the keeper of our memories. More than seventy years later, it is still our nation's best museum, a place that teaches our children of the unspeakable realities of war and the wounds that were sustained in the cause of peace. I believe that we should explore the building of an Australian War Cemetery in Canberra, in the tradition of the Arlington National Cemetery in Virginia, outside Washington DC. Such a cemetery would be a fitting partner for the Australian War Memorial, a piece of ground hallowed by death and gallantry and by those we owe so much, in the heart of our nation. The Australian War Cemetery would be a place of pilgrimage based here, on our own Australian soil.

Defence and national security must be above partisan politics, even if it will always be an intensely important public policy conversation. Under my leadership, Labor has consistently sought to build bipartisanship on national security issues. Keeping Australians safe transcends politics. Labor recognises that no individual and no party has a monopoly on patriotism, or a unique love of our country, or care for the safety of our citizens. We all enjoy the rights and liberties of a safe, tolerant and peaceful democracy—equally. And we all have an equal responsibility to uphold them, to defend them and to preserve the security of our nation. Building the capabilities—human and technological—that enable the ADF to achieve what a government asks of it is necessarily a task that spans decades. It requires foresight and determination. The defence of Australia is a sacred duty of national government. As prime minister, I will uphold that duty every day I serve.

9

CHANGING POLITICS

L ABOR IS THE underdog at the next federal election. We will be trying to achieve something that hasn't happened in eighty years. Yet I believe we can win and must win. Millions of Australians need a Labor government in Canberra, and now, not in three years' time. My party has learnt the hard lessons of the defeat we experienced at the 2013 federal election. The entire ALP—our members, the party organisation and the caucus—have faced up to what went wrong, unified and put things right. Labor is ready to govern again.

I am proud of the achievements of the Rudd and Gillard governments and the work I contributed. I will always be proud of being a part of building the NDIS. As Financial Services Minister, I oversaw the increase in the compulsory superannuation contribution from 9 to 12 per cent, potentially adding to the retirement incomes of 8.4 million Australians, though the increase was regrettably frozen at 9.5 per cent by the Liberals after the 2013 election. I passed legislation putting a cap on interest rates charged by unscrupulous payday lenders, delivered improved governance of the financial planning industry, and oversaw the extension of flood insurance coverage from 3 to 83 per cent nationally. In the months leading up to the 2013 election, I helped negotiate the passage of the government's Gonski education reforms, which provided needs-based funding across Australian schools, giving every child in every school a better start in life. Yet it's no secret that leadership instability cruelled the Labor Party during a portion of its last period in office. The 2010 and 2013 leadership changes were, however, different. In 2010, I was a parliamentary secretary in my first term. I wasn't trying to throw my weight around. The journalist David Marr has told me that my Labor colleagues were surprised by how quiet I was in caucus. In fact, I was completely immersed in the disability portfolio. My view was that in my first term as an MP I was there to watch and learn, and to work hard. The decision to replace Kevin Rudd with Julia Gillard in June 2010 was spontaneous and supported by an overwhelming majority of Labor MPs. Most members of the Labor caucus were chafing under his leadership style. There was a deep wellspring of discontent; however it was not an organised change of leadership. To the best of my understanding, Julia only made up her mind to accept the MPs' endorsement at the last minute. I formed a strong view only in the last few days before the challenge. The truth of the matter is that by the night of 23 June, the leadership contest had already been decided in Julia's favour: if she nominated, she was going to win. I have no doubt she had more than 80 votes in a caucus of 102. And yes, I would have cast my vote for her. It turned out not to be necessary when Kevin, realising he faced likely defeat, resigned the next day. As I have said many times before, I can see in hindsight that the rapid change was not adequately explained to the public.

The 2013 situation was different for the Labor Party. In Labor's second term, I became a minister and was later appointed to cabinet in December 2011. By this time, too, my position in the party had changed. I was by then more deeply engaged in every matter of the government, rather than just my own portfolio. I was one of Julia's strongest supporters when in 2012 Kevin began to mount a challenge and again, in early 2013, when Julia called a spill and no-one else stood. Gradually, I took on more responsibility. By the winter of 2013 I recognised that the government's problems were being keenly felt in the electorate. I could not remain apart. In changing my position, I wanted to be open about it. So, before the final caucus ballot in June 2013, I announced my intention to cast a vote for Kevin. I did not make this decision easily. It was the product of much thought, and I do not resile from it. I did it because I had a deeper obligation to Australia than any particular individual in the Labor Party. Australia needs a strong Labor Party. Electoral annihilation in 2013 for Labor would have wrecked this country—Medicare would have been destroyed and an even more savage budget than the 2014 offering would have been produced. Under Kevin, however, on election day we managed to hold onto fifty-five seats. There's no doubt that Kevin's restored leadership helped to save the furniture. In deciding to support Kevin I had formed the view that we needed to give ourselves a chance of being able to be competitive on the other side of the 2013 election. I knew that I would pay a political price. Nonetheless I found the experience very hard personally, because I was closer to Julia than to Kevin. But the long-term interests of our nation and of my party ultimately had to take precedence.

The Labor Party is united. It is always incumbent on caucus members to remember why they're there and who they're there for. Under my leadership, federal Labor has taken its responsibility to be an alternative government as seriously as our duty to be a strong Opposition. It is significant that I am the first leader of the federal Labor Party to serve in that position for a full term since Kim Beazley occupied the role between 1998 and 2001. But Labor cannot rest on its laurels. We don't need revolutionary reform; however there are important, practical ways by which Labor can change the way it does politics.

Money spent wisely—on education, health, infrastructure, childcare and a range of other necessities—can empower people and change lives.

For all of my thirty-one years in the ALP, I've been a moderate. I began in Young Labor as a member of the Labor Unity faction—Centre Unity nowadays. Factions within the Labor Party have long attracted bad press, sometimes justifiably so. I think it is simplistic, however, to reduce the organisation of a party into factions. Political factions have always been a feature of parliamentary politics. Their basic role is to bring individuals together around a common political purpose. In workplaces, sporting organisations and elsewhere in everyday life people tend to organise in this very manner. In my experience of Labor Party affairs, I've found that factions work with each other vastly more than they ever work against each other.

Factions can give leaders the best possible chance to advance a unified policy agenda. Factions aren't unique to the ALP. There are factions in the Liberal Party and even the Greens Party. The difference is that the Liberal factionalism is often based around a cult of personality and less around a genuine contest of ideas.

I said earlier that my political motto is national interest first, party second, faction third. Excessive factionalism is damaging to political parties and you will often see it at work in youth wings. I probably indulged in a bit of it in my youth: you tend to imitate the conflict of your elders without quite understanding the basis for it. Labor's factions work best when they're a fulcrum for ideas and debates. They operate at their worst when they act as a patronage machine to promote mediocre people. As federal leader I don't think factionally and I don't attend faction meetings. I meet with representatives of the left and right. My job as leader is, in part, to mediate and conciliate internal disagreements where they arise. The Cold War propelled me to one side of the labour movement. That is long gone and I believe that ALP members shouldn't have to belong to a faction to contribute to debate or progress in the party. Younger members especially should be encouraged to work collectively across the groupings and not adhere slavishly to a factional line.

I'm mindful of the drift in recent years of some Labor supporters to the Greens Party. Labor will not win those people back by out-Greening the Greens. I attracted criticism in the lead up to the party's national conference in July 2015, arguing the case for a future Labor government having the option of turning back asylum-seeker boats. I will not go along with any policy settings that would encourage people to put their families onto unsafe boats and risk drowning at sea. I will not live in an intellectually dishonest world where I ignore such happenings. All statements and all policies have consequences. I support regional processing, working in partnership with our neighbours, especially Indonesia. Above all, we have to ensure the dangerous voyage between Java and Christmas Island remains closed. This does not, however, justify the extended detention of asylum seekers on Manus and Nauru. As a prosperous, safe democracy and a leader in our region, Australia can do better and do more to assist genuine refugees. A newly elected Labor government will double Australia's humanitarian intake to 27 000 a year by 2025, and boost funding to the UNHCR to make our nation one of its top five contributors. We will also remove children from detention, restore access to the Refugee Review Tribunal and work with our international partners to implement independent oversight of every Australian-funded facility. Australia is a nation writ large because of migration. We should never forget the debt we owe to generations of migrants and refugees, who in seeking a better life have enriched the lives of us all. Unlike our conservative opponents, we do not play the politics of fear or use labels to denigrate desperate people or posture like the Greens Party. My position won the day, after we reached agreement in the best Labor tradition, through an honest, passionate and open debate. The speeches from that day are all on YouTube—I'd encourage you to watch the contributions, from both sides of the argument. You will see why Labor conferences matter.

Unlike the Greens Party, our conference is held in broad daylight. In stark contrast to all of our rival political parties, Labor has not stood still. Labor has taken realistic, practical steps along the party reform path. We have changed the method by which we elect our federal parliamentary leader, with immediate benefits. The revolving door model of leadership is over. I think we struck an appropriate balance between the rights of party members to have a say over the leadership and the right of the caucus to elect the man or woman with whom they will need to work in Parliament. In pursuit of my aim to broaden the Labor Party's membership base, the national conference removed the requirement that it be compulsory to belong to a union to join the ALP. When I took over the Labor Party, we had 43 000 members. We have now increased membership to nearly 60 000 members. I would like to see a greater say for the rank and file in preselections across Australia. Of course, there is more to be done to make Labor more reflective of the nation at large. Importantly, Labor has set a target that half of our elected members of Parliament within the next ten years will be women. And we are committed to increasing the number of Indigenous Australians in federal Parliament.

The ALP cannot afford to be inwardly focused. Arguing about the future is our way of dealing with our critics on the left as well as the right. We are the champions of the jobs of the future. We are out there arguing for 50 per cent renewable energy. We have said Australia should be a republic within ten years. We have said 50 per cent of MPs should be women. These are ideals whose time had well and truly come. As I said at the outset of this book, if you present Australians with the arguments, the options and some respect, most people will respond thoughtfully. This is the only way in which we can collectively change politics.

The concerning state of the nation's finances has driven Labor's policy work in Opposition. We have been upfront and honest with Australians about our plans, and we have engaged in a real national conversation. I care about how money is spent because money spent wisely—on education, health, infrastructure, childcare and a range of other necessities—can empower people and change lives. The Coalition has more than doubled the deficit since the last election. Labor spends taxpayers' money better than the Coalition. I know this because I was a member of the government that not only steered our nation through the GFC and secured our AAA credit rating from each of the major credit agencies for the first time in Australia's history. A Shorten Labor government will do everything in its powers to repair the Commonwealth budget bottom line—fairly, responsibly, and with a view to the best interests of all Australians. Restoring the Budget to a sustainable footing is essential to promoting growth, boosting productivity and securing jobs beyond the mining boom. That's why we have become the first federal Opposition in history to publicly table the fiscal impact of all our policies—each and every one of our policy commitments has been fully costed and fully funded. We will be relentless in our search for a stronger budget and a budget that serves the common good.

A sustainable budget must involve all Australians paying their fair share. Excessive subsidies and concessions must be excised from the taxation system in the interests of all. Marty Feldstein, former chair of US president Ronald Reagan's

Council of Economic Advisors and one of the world's leading economists, has pointed out that:

> reducing [tax] subsidies ... is really cutting government spending. The resulting deficit reductions show up on the revenue side of the budget, but the economic effect is to cut government spending ... Anyone opposed to government spending should favor removing these subsidies from the tax code.

The Liberals may not like hearing this advice from a Republican, yet this is how fiscal responsibility works. To that end, a Shorten Labor government will ensure that only newly built homes purchased after 1 July 2017 can be negatively geared. Existing investors will not be affected by the changes. Thousands of young Australians will be one step closer to the dream of owning their own home. Analysis by the McKell Institute, reported in February 2016, suggests our changes to negative gearing may create up to 25 000 new jobs in construction, which in turn will increase the nation's housing supply. The budget is being bled dry by distortions. During its time in office the Howard government expanded the capital gains tax discount. Today 70 per cent of capital gains tax discounts are being used by the top 10 per cent of income earners. The capital gains discount cost is growing, on average, at 8 per cent per annum over the forward estimates. This is a significantly faster rate of growth than funding accorded to research, universities, vocational education and training, and schools. This is unsustainable and unfair. A government I lead will halve the capital gains tax deduction from 50 per cent to 25 per cent in order to remove the overly generous taxation treatment of capital gains generated through growing asset prices as opposed to earnings, wages and salaries earned through work. Reducing these tax subsidies will cut government spending by $32 billion over ten years. Our overall improvements to the budget total $100 billion. Labor will also take steps to address the outrage of multinational tax avoidance whereby one in four companies earning more than $100 million dollars a year managed to pay no tax at all. One of the techniques they used to do this involves shifting profits from their Australian offices to offshore havens having disguised them as a loan, or a payment for services because these attract a favourable tax treatment under the law. This is wrong, it is unfair and it is unsustainable. If implemented, our taxation and revenue saving measures will be the most important structural budget reforms undertaken in fifteen years.

Governments cannot solve every problem. Canberra is not the font of all policy wisdom. Great public policy is not confined to public sector–based solutions. Superannuation is a great example of this principle, and potentially so is reducing carbon pollution. Non-government service delivery is another area of promise. The ultimate aim of the NDIS is to allow Australians living with a disability greater freedom of choice, rather leaving them as prisoners of impersonal bureaucracy. Any government I lead will operate in a collegial, consultative manner where cabinet decision-making processes and caucus debate are taken seriously. To me decentralising power is more than a noble ambition or slogan. It's a style of leadership that works. People have to be involved and feel involved. Leaders have got to be conciliators and negotiators. They have to be people who bring others with them. I don't believe in a super-hero theory of leadership or acting out some messianic leader fantasy. I believe a leader is the chairman of the board at one level and a coach and an enabler at another level—getting the best out of a team. When I look at our Labor team I see great ability and passion—Tanya Plibersek, Chris Bowen, Penny Wong, Stephen Conroy, Jenny Macklin, Anthony Albanese, Tony Burke, Brendan O'Connor, Kim Carr, Richard Marles, Joel Fitzgibbon, Mark Dreyfus, Jason Clare, Mark Butler, Kate Ellis and former chief minister of the ACT, Katy Gallagher. All bring real-life experience, as well as previous cabinet experience, and many have directly managed budgets in organisations as diverse as small business, large associations and listed corporations. And as Tanya Plibersek has pointed out, it is significant that every member of Labor's leadership group is raising young children. Key decisions will be made using that prism.

Often, our nation gets nostalgic about the way politics played out in the past. I do not subscribe to the assertion that it's more difficult to make things happen in today's political world. It's probably true that today's media environment is tougher, with a constant media cycle. I genuinely believe it is still possible to sell necessary, practical change in contemporary Australia. I did it in the hundreds of enterprise agreements I negotiated during my time at the AWU—convincing workers to embrace flexibility; convincing companies to pay their employees more money than they wanted to; trying to identify the value in the business and how people contribute; and then making sure all got their fair share. We convinced racing authorities to do more for jockeys. I convinced the company building the Eastlink freeway in Melbourne to pay their workforce the highest civil construction rates in Australia, in exchange for more flexible timing on when people had days off. It was a matter of finding what the value is. It was all about multiple-issue negotiations, just as it is in politics. If you can create value, if you can say there are multiple issues here, you won't make everyone happy but you can go a lot further.

During the ALP national conference in 2015, that was how the vote on marriage equality proceeded. The socially conservative–minded in the party didn't want to give up the existing policy of guaranteeing MPs a conscience vote on the issue. Rainbow Labor, the party's marriage equality advocacy group, wanted a free vote replaced immediately by the usual caucus practice that requires all MPs to vote strictly in line with party policy. We found a middle way. The outcome was that we kept the conscience vote longer than Rainbow Labor wanted, for the next two parliaments. Meanwhile, the social conservatives accepted the position that there should eventually be a binding vote on the basis that it was likely that marriage equality would happen in the next three or four years anyway. While it wasn't a perfect outcome, it achieved consensus and real progress. The point is this: if you want to advocate change, begin with the world as it is—where people are in the here and now.

The real challenge in our politics is ordinary citizens don't see any reason to get involved because they feel it is disconnected from their daily lives and they think they can't change anything anyway, so why bother? Too many Australians didn't bother to lodge a ballot at the last election: 400 000 Australians aged between 18 and 24 failed to enrol to vote between the 2010 and 2013 elections. We need to think about engaging people earlier and keeping them engaged. To that end, last year I opened up a debate about extending the right to vote to Australians from the age of 16—people who work, who pay tax, are trusted to drive a car or fly a plane and serve in our military. We've seen in recent years a rise in online activism through such organisations as Get Up! I helped establish Get Up! in 2005. Its aim was to revitalise grassroots politics. Yet sharing a graphic or signing a petition is not necessarily full engagement. Our democracy is precious. Politicians are its custodians. It is incumbent on us to promote a more vibrant, stronger civil society. That requires leadership.

Not every great reform or idea originates from one side of politics. I don't hate Liberals. I'm not motivated to pursue a career in politics to stop my opponents from acquiring power. I do oppose a lot of what they do or want to do. That's not because I'm from one tribe and they're from the other. On one issue, I did respect Prime Minister John Howard: he was brave when he tightened the nation's gun laws in 1996. Yet under his leadership, national productivity slumped. Because of the Howard government's sit-back-and-relax attitude, we missed the first mining boom completely and embedded structural deficits. As a result, Australia does not value-add as much as it should. Advanced manufacturing did not advance under Howard and Costello, and nor did our universities. The position of women didn't greatly advance. Inequality increased. For all their talk of tax reform, they left office as one of the highest-taxing governments in Australian history. The Howard government did three key things: it introduced the GST, albeit at a rate of 10 per cent and exempting basic foods; oversaw the gun buy-back laws; and intervened in East Timor.

They did all of that and not much else. Let us never forget that the Howard/Costello government frittered away the dividend of the mining boom. It was fixated on political survival rather than a future-focused national reform agenda.

In Opposition, Labor's policy development process has departed from the old politics. We have been bold, putting policy ahead of politics so that in government we can build the strongest economy and promote the good society. We are not a small target and nor would I want to lead such a party. A number of our ideas have come from discussions with people outside of Labor circles. We have reached out to a number of think tanks and various experts, and drawn on the best international experience. Our policies have been worked up in a steady and methodical manner, tested rigorously, and properly costed and funded. We have returned politics to the community, engaging in thousands of conversations with Australians from all walks of life, whether through traditional policy forums or virtually.

The fatal flaw in putting politics first is that once a government's ascendancy is lost, structures and processes of policy formulation and implementation cannot suddenly be rehabilitated: they need to have been in place from the beginning. Long-term social and economic reform requires a broad, coherent set of policies, drawn from extensive consultation, and based on the widest possible consensus in and outside of Parliament.

That's the type of national government I intend to lead.

10

REAL LEADERSHIP

JUST AS OUR time on this Earth is finite, all governments have a limited life span. It's vital that parliamentarians elected by their fellow Australians don't waste a moment and don't waste a sentence once they've taken office. A new government should come armed with a well-thought-out, well-articulated plan and a set of processes for office that does not assume immortality. It must be fuelled with a burning ambition that the programs it creates will become permanent national institutions. With the support of the Australian people, I commit to measure my achievements in terms of policy impact and rebuilding a sense of national unity.

There are ongoing responsibilities of government business that require leadership. Cabinet processes have fallen away on the watch of both the Abbott and Turnbull governments. In 2015, the nation was treated to a near-complete breakdown of cabinet over the proposal to strip dual-nationality terrorists of their Australian citizenship. There was no proper cabinet submission; other ministers were not consulted by the prime minister or the immigration minister—it was an ambush. These rules are not pointless bureaucracy. Process counts. In my decision-making, I have always consulted with the widest array of people and will continue to do so as prime minister and chair of cabinet. My shadow cabinet has operated along these lines for more than two and a half years. My belief is that effective leadership does not mean accumulating power. On the contrary, it has been my experience that devolving power has the potential to produce superior process and policy.

National leadership requires a vision for our national identity. John Howard used to say, with no small measure of pride, that his time in office put an end to the 'perpetual seminar' on Australia's national identity. However, no leader can 'end' a conversation about our nation's sense of self. The next generation will have a contribution to make on this question as the country continues to evolve. Talking about our nation's past is not navel-gazing. Done respectfully, it is a way to examine our past practices and our values, and to advance the country. And real patriots know that until a nation includes everyone— in its historical considerations, in its present-day society, its economy and in its constitutional arrangements—then there is always more to do.

I have long supported an Australian republic. Right now, the sticking point among republicans is how to select a president: through a popular vote or some form of selection. The establishment of a college of state and territory governors from whom a president could be drawn could overcome the direct-electionists' opposition to the previous minimalist model in which a head of state was to be appointed by parliamentarians.

One of the key lessons from 1999 is we need a clear process, owned by the Australian people.

Federation is instructive. After the failure of the 1891 Constitutional Convention, the Victorian John Quick came up with the idea of an 'enabling' bill to be passed by each of the colonial parliaments, laying out a clear timetable for Federation. This generated new momentum for the 'Yes' cause. Granted, there will be a range of complex legal, constitutional and policy questions to sort through. However a clear process is essential. One sequence might involve the staging of a constitutional convention, followed by a plebiscite to gauge popular support and to choose the preferred model, and then a referendum to formally enact constitutional change within ten years.

> *Real action is needed to address the racism, injustice, poverty and disadvantage that afflict the lives of the First Australians.*

I also believe we must end the 'great Australian silence' that remains in our founding document. We must recognise the traditional owners of our continent in our nation's constitution. I am confident this is the view of the great, generous majority of Australians, just as it was in the iconic 1967 referendum. Like the republic, there will be always be a small number more interested in railing against imagined 'political correctness' and reopening a new front in the 'history wars' than playing a constructive role in our national conversation. That's their prerogative and, I would submit, their loss. My government's focus will concern itself with crafting a broad consensus—across Parliament and around the nation—for concrete and meaningful change. Any proposal for constitutional change we take to the Australian people must be owned and shaped by Aboriginal and Torres Strait Islander peoples and their community-based representative organisations. In that way, we can make the Recognition moment as uplifting as Kevin Rudd's 2009 apology to the stolen generations; as honest as Paul Keating's 1992 Redfern Park speech; and as unstoppable as Gough Whitlam pouring a handful of Daguragu soil through Vincent Lingiari's hands in 1975. I'm so proud to have Pat Dodson—a great Australian I first met in my union days travelling through the Kimberley—on-board as Labor's new senator for Western Australia. I cannot think of a better qualified Indigenous leader to have alongside my colleagues and me, and our Indigenous communities in the trenches as we prosecute a war against poverty and discrimination that simply has to be won. In regards to Indigenous recognition and the republic, there will be people who say these are second-order issues that can wait for a better time, at a later date. That's not a new argument—or a strong one.

My approach to reconciliation does not end with constitutional recognition. Real action is needed to address the racism, injustice, poverty and disadvantage that afflict the lives of the First Australians. When Indigenous people die ten years earlier than non-Indigenous Australians, we need to offer more than recognition. When Australia is the only developed nation in the world where trachoma is endemic, we need to change more than our constitution. When half of the young people in juvenile detention are Aboriginal and Torres Strait Islander people, when 2 per cent of our population makes up more than a quarter of our prison population, when an Indigenous man leaving school is more likely to go to jail than university, we must do more than correct historical injustice. This is why Labor built the Closing the Gap framework and set clear targets and timetables around early childhood education; Year 12 completion; halving the employment gap by 2018; halving the mortality gap for children under five; and closing the life expectancy gap by 2031. The first meeting of the Council of Australian Governments (COAG) convened under a Shorten Labor government will work on justice targets. We will work closely with state and local governments, through law enforcement agencies, and departments of corrections and community services. We will be guided by the people who live the reality of the justice gap: community leaders, Elders and Aboriginal representative organisations. Crime and incarceration affect the safety of the whole community, and the solution belongs to the whole community. I don't pretend to have all the answers, or believe that governments can resolve every issue. There has been enough of that—enough imposed solutions creating new problems. Instead, we need to recognise that the best plans and policies depend upon fundamental respect for Aboriginal and Torres Strait Islander peoples. Empowering people has guided my whole working life, and I remain convinced that the best outcomes occur when people are empowered to make decisions over their own lives. Indigenous affairs is no exception.

I've already described my Jesuit education and the social justice values I have drawn from it. In the lead-up to marrying Chloe I converted from Catholic to Anglican. I had come to disagree with the Church on a number of issues: stem-cell research, the right of women to control their own bodies, priestly marriage and, more lately, marriage equality. The subject of denomination was closer to Chloe's heart, so we

tied the knot at St Thomas's Anglican Church in my electorate. But I did not shed my Jesuit values. In October 2014, I
delivered a speech to the Australian Christian Lobby in which
I supported marriage equality. That was regarded as the most
newsworthy part of my talk, although I was merely laying out
the reason why I believe that marriage equality is compatible
with my faith, not trying to be provocative to a roomful of
fellow Christians. There is much sensitivity in the political
world—and parts of the wider community—about how much
religious faith should be acknowledged, much less discussed,
by politicians. To some degree, that's understandable: faith is
intensely personal. Many political players judge that it's best to
steer clear of religion altogether. It's fair to say that this view is
more prevalent on my side of politics. Some of it lies in history.
Large segments of the Catholic Church broke away from Labor
in the 1950s, and for a long time some congregations were
actively dissuaded from the pulpit from voting ALP. There's
also a view on the progressive side of politics that religion is
the preserve of political and social conservatives. That's not
how I see it.

In the Sermon on the Mount, Jesus proclaims that universal
love, tolerance and service underpin his Gospel. He rejects the
empty vengeance of an eye for an eye and tells us instead to
turn the other cheek. Judge not, Jesus tells us: 'For in the same
way you judge others, you will be judged, and with the measure
you use, it will be measured to you'. Above all, he tells us to
love our neighbour as we love ourselves, to treat people as
we would like to be treated. In everything, do to others what
you would have them do to you. When I was at school we were
taught that this was the golden rule. It lay at the heart of the

Jesuit call to be a 'man for others'. I have spent my working life, both representing workers and as a parliamentarian, trying to measure up to this standard of compassion and empathy, to care for the vulnerable, to speak up for the powerless, to reject hatred and intolerance, to help the poor and to pursue the path of peace. None of these virtues belongs to Christianity alone, nor does a belief in social justice necessarily depend upon the teachings of Christ.

When I hear people invoking the scriptures to attack blended families like mine I cannot stay silent. When I see people hiding behind the Bible to insult and demonise people based on who they love I cannot stay silent. When I hear people allege that 'God tells them' that marriage equality is the first step on the road to polygamy, bigamy and bestiality, I cannot stay silent. These prejudices do not reflect the Christian values I believe in. Regrettably, it feeds a perception that Church and faith are somehow incompatible with modern families, with modern life, with modern Australia, and I reject that. Christian values can still guide us in our journey through the modern world. There is nothing old-fashioned about compassion or respect, nothing outdated in the idea of seeking peace, caring for others, contributing to society and loving your family. It has never been more relevant, never more important.

That's some of what I told the Australian Christian Lobby. I also expanded on my position on marriage equality: 'Friends, if we can agree on these things, if we agree that our duty is to help the vulnerable, to speak up for the powerless, to gather in those who feel marginalised and excluded—I wonder how we can continue to draw a line based on who people love? How can compassion, charity, love, recognition and endorsement continue to be restricted to heterosexual Australia and the nuclear family? I believe in God and I believe in marriage equality under the civil law of the Commonwealth of Australia.' I went on to say that for some people of faith, marriage equality is a most vexed question. It is one of the reasons Labor has made marriage equality a conscience vote in previous parliaments. At its heart, marriage equality is a question of legal recognition and legal support for couples committed to each other, regardless of their gender. My reasons for voting for change are based upon the broad ideal of equality—an Australia that includes everyone. Whatever our religious views about marriage, and whatever our social views about how best to raise and educate children, we have to change this law which discriminates against adult couples on the basis of who they love. At the July 2015 ALP national conference, I promised to move for marriage equality within the first hundred days after the next election should Labor win office, rather than engage in a divisive, harmful $160 million taxpayer-funded opinion poll.

Democracy works only when the people and leaders trust each other. You cannot underestimate the value of trust. There's also the element of negotiation: how do you create value in a negotiation? Single-issue negotiations are diabolical because there has to be a winner and a loser. The key is to understand when and where interests diverge on a broader scale. My first instinct when negotiating is to understand where the other party is coming from and where I'm coming from. Then you think about whether there is some shared interest at work, or at least the possibility of multi-issue negotiation, where both parties can have a win. Let me give an example. As a union official, I negotiated annualised salaries for members. The win for them was that they would be guaranteed more than just thirty-eight hours a week pay. It could be that they got six hours of overtime built into their weekly pay, or a couple of hours at time-and-a-half and four at double-time. This meant that effectively they would be working forty-four hours a week and be paid for forty-nine hours. Even better, because this was now their actual rate of pay, they would receive superannuation benefits on the latter figure, whereas until then they had only been getting super based on hours worked. The appeal for the employer was capping overtime—the job had to be done within forty-four hours and no more. The employee also got certainty—a better lifestyle and a guaranteed income. It also gave the employee an incentive to complete the work in less time. If they could do the job in forty-three hours, they would be paid for an hour they were not there. Some employers struggled with that idea, just as some members struggled with the idea of their hours being capped. But if you can create a situation where you incentivise getting the job done rather than the number of hours you're there, based upon which hour is of more value, it creates shared value.

A recent example shows what can happen when politicians do not look for shared value. In the 2015 discussions regarding the China–Australia Free Trade Agreement struck between the government and China, the government ignored Labor's concerns about labour protections. Its position was hard-line: we will not change the agreement. Our position was that there were other things it could change to bring about the result we were after, chiefly the *Migration Act*. That way, our concerns could be met and the free trade agreement would be untouched. The government was unable to sell any change to the country. It had been battered by bad polls for a very long time. It should have been able to see that it was not in a healthy place electorally, and we were offering to give it what it wanted: the passage of the agreement. However the government was pathologically addicted to fighting us. Our issues on labour protection and the need for market testing were legitimate. So what was the real issue here: for the government was it getting a trade agreement implemented or fighting the Opposition? And was our issue getting a trade agreement or just simply saying 'no'? What was needed was for both sides to identify the shared interest. The government was reduced to telling fibs about Labor's stance, claiming that we opposed the agreement. Tellingly, the government eventually accepted our amendments, enshrining labour market testing: the *Migration Act* now mandates employers to advertise locally before recruiting Chinese workers. It was a tortuous path to shared value, but as a result of our efforts, the China–Australia Free Trade Agreement is a superior agreement.

Another example: for ten years, successive governments have been trying to work out regulations for disability housing in public buildings. As parliamentary secretary, I brought together people with disabilities, architects, the Real Estate Institute, the Housing Institute, and human rights groups. We came to form a compact about more liveable housing. We talked through what we actually wanted, without recourse to regulation, and we set some new standards, which were agreed to voluntarily. None of that was easy. I gathered these groups together at Kirribilli and just let them sit together and talk. That talk led to results.

Bringing people together is the best way I know of finding solutions to difficult problems. I have already proposed that a national summit be held early in the life of my government, should I get to head one. I certainly think there is a need for a national crisis summit on family violence, one that would bring together the voices of survivors, the police, the experts and families, and lead to practical outcomes. A summit cannot be a whiteboard session that begins with a blank whiteboard. A government has to arrive with a view—that's what Hawke did in 1983—and have that view tested by the participants. Another view may emerge—a counter-view or a hybrid form—but you have to go in having a view. A summit is not necessarily about working out the particular path: it's about working out the shared interest, an agreement and generating momentum. It also serves as a reminder that governments of all political persuasions cannot possibly know everything about everything; good ideas can come from anywhere and are always worth considering.

In this changing world our nation needs a more flexible and consensus-driven politics. We need consensus not as an end in itself, but because the challenges ahead of Australia are complex. The lasting prosperity with fairness our country deserves requires difficult decisions—only consensus can get us there. Only a new consensus—a renewed politics of the common good—can lead us towards the new economic growth we need beyond the mining boom. Only a politics of the common good can drive innovation and productivity, and create a highly skilled, educated workforce that will be able to enjoy the stable, secure, well-paid jobs of the future. The same is true of the challenge of repairing the budget bottom line in the fairest way possible, and fixing our tax system and retire-ment policies. The eternal fight against inequality in all its guises—from the rights of women to equal marriage—taking action on climate change, and working towards real recon-ciliation with Australia's first peoples, each of these challenges requires a commitment to the common good. A common good does not just happen and will, by necessity, make demands on all of us. A renewed politics of the common good means bringing together people of goodwill. I know that getting people of goodwill in the same room always beats goodwill meetings in separate rooms. We need to think about national politics in precisely the same way. We should encourage dialogue, nego-tiation and compromise, whether it is in our communities or in our schools, workplaces, marketplaces, boardrooms or our parliaments.

Only a new consensus—a renewed politics of the common good—can lead us towards the new economic growth we need beyond the mining boom.

My approach is necessary not because I'm some sort of good bloke or because I won't fight when necessary. It is absolutely essential for our nation because I know that across the span of my professional life it has worked. Real leadership is recom-mending to your own a course of action that they might not automatically accept. It means empowering people rather than doing things to and for them. It is about saying hard things to powerful vested interests when necessary. It means listen-ing to others. It means identifying, embracing and adapting to change wherever it is desirable and making change work for all. It means being brave enough to oppose change where it is unfair, where it is not pursued collaboratively in the national interest and when it is not compatible with the Australian Way. I believe that this is a time for all Australians to look ahead with a renewed sense of national confidence and openness, conscious of our past yet not weighed down by it. We must be ambitious out of necessity. We must rediscover our ability to work for the common good—employees, unionists, businesses of all shapes and sizes, governments and the many diverse people and communities across this country all pulling together—and place this creed at the heart of everything we do. Nothing less than the future of our nation depends on it.